ALSO BY KAREN BLUMENTHAL

Bootleg: Murder, Moonshine, and the Lawless Years of Prohibition

Steve Jobs: The Man Who Thought Different

TOMMY
THE GUN THAT CHANGED AMERICA

KAREN BLUMENTHAL

ROARING BROOK PRESS  New York

Published by Roaring Brook Press
Roaring Brook Press is a division of Holtzbrinck Publishing Holdings Limited Partnership
175 Fifth Avenue, New York, New York 10010
macteenbooks.com

Library of Congress Cataloging-in-Publication Data

Blumenthal, Karen.
    Tommy : the gun that changed America / Karen Blumenthal. — First edition.
      pages cm
    Includes bibliographical references and index.
    ISBN 978-1-62672-084-8 (hardcover) — ISBN 978-1-62672-085-5 (e-book)
    1. Thompson submachine gun—History—Juvenile literature.   I. Title.
    UF620.T5B55 2015
    683.4'22—dc23

                                                    2014040642

Roaring Brook Press books may be purchased for business or promotional use. For information on
bulk purchases please contact Macmillan Corporate and Premium Sales Department at
(800) 221-7945 x5442 or by email at specialmarkets@macmillan.com.

First edition 2015
Printed in the United States of America

1   3   5   7   9   10   8   6   4   2

To Meredith and Brian

A 1931 *Popular Science* cover highlights a new kind of cavalry, a military "gasoline brigade" that includes men on motorcycles with Tommy guns attached.

CONTENTS

LOCKED AND LOADED

JOHN ENZ NEVER HAD A CHANCE.

The thirty-two-year-old driver arrived early to work on October 14, 1926, ready to go. His boss sent him out on a new route, driving a U.S. mail truck loaded with cash through Elizabeth, New Jersey. An assistant joined him, and a police escort on a motorcycle followed behind.

Around 9:20 a.m., two cars suddenly pulled beside the mail truck and motorcycle. Before anyone could react, a single shooter's bullets filled the air.

Enz was hit in the head and crumpled to the ground. His assistant managed to fire a couple of shots from his pistol before he was shot in the wrist and the hip.

A second gunman shot the policeman.

While onlookers ducked to avoid the flying bullets, crooks jumped from both cars and used large bolt cutters to slash the wire protecting the mail truck's contents. They grabbed several bags from the truck,

The damaged U.S. postal truck

Crowds gather at Sixth Street and Elizabeth Avenue, where John Enz was killed during a postal-truck robbery.

stuffed them into their cars, and roared away. Within minutes, they had escaped with more than $150,000 in cash—nearly $2 million in today's money—which was meant to pay workers at the nearby Singer Sewing Machine Company.

The crooks left behind a dying John Enz, father of a three-year-old son; his assistant and police escort were badly injured.

In their rush, the bandits left something else: their unusual, fast-firing weapon, a Thompson submachine gun.

Until that day, the Thompson gun was little known on the East Coast. But for more than a year, the weapon, developed to help American soldiers in trench warfare, had been making a roar in Chicago. There, gangsters were turning it against one another in clashes over territory.

Just days before the Elizabeth robbery, two well-known Chicago gangsters were killed and three others, including a popular criminal lawyer, were injured in a machine-gun shooting so gory that it turned the pavement red. For the most part, the powerful weapon had been seen as Chicago's problem, and a gangster problem at that. Now the battlefield was in New Jersey, and the targets were police and employees of the U.S. mail.

News of the shooting—in broad daylight on a regular city street—rattled the nation. President Calvin Coolidge devoted a cabinet meeting to discussing how his government could protect the mail. Others shuddered to think that more crooks might use "the most dangerous small arm in the world." A commentator in the *New York Times* noted, "America's criminals have turned the deadliest weapons of modern warfare against society."

As dozens of law enforcement officers fanned out around Elizabeth to find the seven bandits involved, newpapers and magazines worldwide wondered how such a weapon could not only be legal, but also freely available at regular sporting-goods and hardware stores.

John Taliaferro Thompson, the gun's creator and namesake, was distressed that the elegant and destructive weapon he intended for war was now in the hands of criminals. After one Chicago shooting, he paced up and down his New York office racked with concern.

"What can we do?" he asked. "What can we do?"

Indeed, what could anyone do?

CHAPTER 1

CONCEPTION

THE GUN THAT SHOOK ELIZABETH, New Jersey, was roughly the size of a new baby, eight-and-a-half pounds unloaded and 23.2 inches long without its stock. In less than a minute, it could spit out 800 bullets if you could feed it ammunition fast enough.

It was, without a doubt, an impressive little killing machine.

Sleek, compact, and efficient, the Thompson submachine gun was a new kind of weapon for modern times, developed by a career army man dedicated to providing U.S. soldiers with proper arms and ammunition. But the gun also had a heritage, descending from an expanding line of powerful military firearms. Probably its most direct ancestor was the Gatling gun, the first truly workable machine gun capable of rapid and regular fire.

Just after the Civil War began, Richard Jordan Gatling, a medical doctor, developed his gun with the hope that it could save lives. He later wrote to a friend: "It occurred to me that if I could invent a

A police detective displays the fast-firing Thompson gun that the Elizabeth mail bandits left behind.

A hand crank loaded and turned the barrels of the Gatling gun, the first truly workable machine gun.

machine—a gun—which could by rapidity of fire enable one man to do as much battle duty as a hundred, that it would, to a great extent, supersede the necessity of large armies . . ." That, Gatling thought, would greatly reduce the number of men who died on the battlefield from injuries and exposure to diseases.

The early Gatling gun was an ingenious and deceptively simple design: Six barrels were clustered in a tight circle. Initially weighing more than 200 pounds, it sat like a miniature cannon between two large wheels and typically was pulled by horses or mules. Several men worked together to operate it, turning a crank that allowed it to load ammunition, fire, and load the next barrel, dispatching as many as 200 bullets a minute. The multiple barrels meant that no one barrel overheated, allowing true continuous firing for the first time.

An early sales brochure touted it as "the most effective implement of warfare ever invented."

Unfortunately for Gatling, the Union army wasn't interested. One reason may have been that Gatling was born in North Carolina and was feared to be a Southern sympathizer. But there were other problems. The army's ordnance department, which was responsible for weapons and ammunition, wasn't the least bit intrigued by newfangled innovations, especially one that was untested in battle. Already, dozens of different weapons were in use. And since the machine gun was the size of a little cannon, it was seen as a piece of artillery—something that should fire big ammunition from a long range far from the front lines. But this one just spit out little bullets, and it jammed easily.

Even more, military leaders deeply distrusted such bullet-spewing machines. A machine gun ran counter to all battlefield tradition. Where was the glory, the heroism, the courage in turning a crank? In the next century, wars would be waged with big bombs, long-range missiles, and drones. But in Gatling's day, military men believed that war should be fought by men, not machines.

A couple of wealthy and forward-thinking Union soldiers bought several Gatling guns themselves and used them in battle. But the army didn't officially adopt the gun until 1866, after the war ended.

The Gatling gun wasn't formally tested in an American battle until 1898. That February, the USS *Maine* exploded in Cuba's Havana Harbor. The disaster was blamed on Spain, which controlled Cuba, Guam, Puerto Rico, and the Philippines. In April, the United States declared war, marking the official start of the Spanish-American War.

Troops and supplies were dispatched to Tampa, Florida, to prepare for war in Cuba. One young second lieutenant, John Henry Parker, arrived eager to challenge the conventional wisdom that modern machine guns couldn't be productive in battle. He was certain they would be more useful on the front lines than back with the cannons and other artillery.

John Henry Parker, around 1898

But Parker had a hard time finding a sympathetic ear. His direct superior told Parker that he simply wasn't interested. Parker created a written proposal and approached a top commander, but he was too busy to hear Parker's plan.

By luck, Parker met the Fifth Army Corps' ordnance officer, John T. Thompson, and made his case while Thompson enjoyed a dish of ice cream.

The thirty-seven-year-old Thompson was up to his ears in arms and ammunition. He had arrived in Tampa in late April to find supply trains backed up for fifty miles. Dozens and dozens of boxes of rifle and revolver cartridges, powder charges, and mortars were arriving daily, without a single mark on the box to describe what was inside. Matching the boxes with invoices that came either days before or after the boxes arrived was a nightmare. But Thompson knew that his arsenal included fifteen never-used Gatling guns, still in their crates.

Thompson told Parker that he, too, had long believed machine guns had a place on the front lines, and he offered to help convince their superiors.

In late May, Parker was allowed to form a small machine-gun unit to operate the Gatlings. A few days later, though, when the Fifth Army Corps began to move out, there was no mention of Parker's Gatling gun group.

Parker again hunted down Thompson, who was desperately trying to get ammunition and equipment to the boat headed to Cuba. Without seeking a commander's approval, Thompson offered Parker a deal. If Parker helped to load more than 500,000 rounds of ammunition onto the train supplying the ship to Cuba, Thompson would sneak on four Gatling guns as well.

The fighting in Cuba started in late June, and the American forces found some of their equipment embarrassingly out of date. The Spaniards had newer rifles and machine guns, while the United States was relying in part on inferior single-shot weapons. The U.S. artillery's black-powder ammunition left tufts of telltale white smoke around American positions, while the Spaniards used smokeless ammunition.

Initially, Parker's battery was held back as the Americans, trying to capture Santiago, faced relentless fire. Finally, Parker got the go-ahead to move his Gatlings up to the front lines. When the Spaniards looked over the trenches to shoot at the advancing American soldiers, Parker's men took aim, firing continuously for several minutes. The enemy "were seen to melt away like a lump of salt in a glass of water," Parker said later.

While the Gatlings provided cover, Teddy Roosevelt and his Rough Riders were able to storm Spanish positions.

"Our artillery, using black powder, had not been able to stand within range of the Spanish rifles," Roosevelt remembered. But then the Gatlings engaged in direct battle.

A soldier uses a Gatling gun in deep grass during the Spanish-American War in Cuba.

When the relentless drumming of the machine guns started, Roosevelt called out to encourage his men: "It's the Gatlings, men! It's our Gatlings."

"Immediately, the troops began to cheer lustily," Roosevelt said, "for the sound was most inspiring."

The entire war lasted just a few weeks. At the end, Spain gave Cuba its independence and Guam and Puerto Rico to the United States. The United States paid $20 million for the Philippines. John Henry Parker earned the nickname "Gatling Gun" Parker for his persistence in taking the Gatlings along.

And John Taliaferro Thompson, now an up-and-coming officer in army ordnance, was convinced his country needed more advanced weapons and ammunition as part of a more thoughtful and well-planned arsenal.

Teddy Roosevelt and his Rough Riders, 1898

Thompson's next assignment was to the Springfield Armory in Massachusetts, where he oversaw development of a new bolt-action rifle, the Springfield M1903, based on a German rifle that had been used in Cuba. The new rifle, which used smokeless ammunition, was known for its exceptional accuracy at long distances, and a variation of it would be used by American troops for the next fifty years.

In late 1903, the War Department asked Thompson and Major Louis A. La Garde, an army surgeon, to combine their experience and lead a series of tests to choose the best pistol bullet for "stopping power and

John Thompson during his army years

shock effect at short ranges." Officials were disturbed that the army's .38-caliber Colt revolvers hadn't done a very effective job in the Philippines during the Spanish-American War. Even when they were shot, some enemy fighters had continued to charge toward American soldiers.

Thompson and La Garde went at their work in a most unusual—and rather unscientific—way. They first rounded up ten cadavers, hung them by their necks so their feet were off the ground, and shot them with various guns loaded with bullets of different sizes, shapes, and weights. They tried to estimate how much each body part swayed when shot. Then they examined each wound to see if bones were broken and how much tissue was damaged.

To test "shock," they tied up cattle and horses headed to slaughter. Initially, they shot the animals several times and then waited to see what happened. When the first animals suffered for longer than expected, they tried a different "quick-fire" method, shooting until the animal collapsed. Wrote La Garde: "The animals invariably dropped to the ground when shot from three to five times with the larger caliber Colt's revolver bullets, and they failed in every instance to drop when as many as ten shots of the smaller jacketed bullets . . . had been delivered against the lungs or abdomen."

The experiments were crude, messy, and inhumane, but they led the pair to a key conclusion: A military pistol or revolver of at least .45-caliber would be the most effective. The bullets used in .45 caliber pistols were shorter and fatter than those used in .30-caliber rifles and moved more slowly when fired. Rather than ripping straight through a person like a smaller bullet, the larger bullet was more likely to lodge in the body, sending a shock through the system. One man who had been accidentally shot in the shoulder by a .45 pistol round described it as if "about a dozen men had rammed him with a telephone pole."

By 1907, Thompson was senior assistant to the army's chief of ordnance, based in Washington, D.C. He urged gunmakers to develop .45-caliber military pistols that could automatically load a new bullet after one was fired so that soldiers could shoot more efficiently. Old-fashioned revolvers required pulling the hammer to load a bullet from the next chamber, which jerked the gun and made staying on target challenging. Reloading the Springfield rifle required moving the bolt up and back. Thompson's work helped lead to the army's adoption of the Colt .45 M1911 automatic pistol as its standard firearm. With each pull of the trigger, the gun reloaded from a seven-bullet magazine, what we call a semiautomatic weapon today. It became an army mainstay for decades.

As a top ordnance officer, Thompson created a detailed plan for increasing weapons manufacturing, ordering ordnance, and issuing supplies so that the United States could quickly equip 500,000 men if war broke out.

He also was an active member of the National Rifle Association, an organization formed in 1871 to improve the marksmanship of potential soldiers through training and shooting contests. The NRA got a boost in 1905 when Congress allowed rifle clubs to buy surplus military arms and ammunition for target practice and competitions, the association's primary focus well into the 1920s. In 1914, Thompson urged rifle practice for high school boys, in hopes that more men would be ready for military duty.

Most of all, Thompson wanted his country to be well prepared and well armed for war. In a 1905 speech in Davenport, Iowa, he told the audience that "extreme humanitarians," such as Russian writer Leo Tolstoy, believed that adding to the weapons arsenal was a bad idea because "the mere possession of the tools of war creates the desire to use them."

But Thompson disagreed. He sided with Teddy Roosevelt, now president of the United States, who believed in the maxim: "In time of peace, prepare for war."

Guns had come a long way since the Civil War. Once, many guns had been made by hand. The development of machine tools in the late 1800s had led to consistent, finely tuned parts and more precise construction. By the last part of the century, guns that used to be made of cast iron were now made from forged steel. That made guns more powerful and accurate and helped encourage the creation of a significant steel industry in the United States.

Still to come, Thompson predicted, were more formidable arms for modern battle, especially automatic weapons, which loaded ammunition on their own and fired a steady stream of lead with a single pull of the trigger.

In 1913, Lieutenent Colonel John Thompson was named a colonel. The magazine *Arms and the Man* applauded his promotion, calling him "an officer of exceptional ability" and a forward thinker "who labors with sound judgment to improve existing conditions." The article also noted that Thompson "has been greatly interested for many years in the discovery of an automatic rifle" and had encouraged gunmakers to develop one.

Like the pistol and revolver, machine guns had improved since the Gatling gun. But Thompson's superiors in the army still saw such guns as accessories rather than core weapons of war. Machine guns were considered "weapons of emergency" to be used only in special situations. The army's drill regulations in 1911 were almost condescending about such weapons, saying, "fire alone cannot be depended upon to stop an attack."

Even more clear: The U.S. Army wasn't going to make any effort to develop a better or lighter machine gun itself.

In 1914, as the First World War was breaking out in Europe, the fifty-three-year-old Colonel Thompson shocked many in the military by retiring from the army. Shortly thereafter, he signed on to help build and run a plant in Eddystone, Pennsylvania, to make Enfield rifles for British soldiers.

The job almost surely paid better than the army, but there was another reason for his departure. Thompson deeply believed American soldiers needed a lightweight, handheld automatic rifle that could deliver a scorching stream of bullets, machine-gun-like, to faraway targets. If there was going to be such a weapon, he concluded, he would have to create it himself.

CHAPTER 2
TRENCH BROOM

JOHN TALIAFERRO THOMPSON had never actually designed a gun before or led the development of one. But as the second child of Julia Maria Taliaferro and Lieutenant Colonel James Thompson, he was born into the military business.

James, a graduate of the United States Military Academy at West Point, New York, was stationed in Texas when his only son entered the world on December 31, 1860, in Newport, Kentucky. The Civil War started soon after, and James fought in several battles with distinction.

As James was posted from place to place, young John moved frequently.

James retired from the military in 1869 because of war-related injuries and taught military science at Indiana University. John attended a preparatory high school program there and then followed his father's path to West Point, graduating eleventh in his class in 1882.

That same year, he married Juliet Estelle Hagans. In 1883, their only child, Marcellus Hagans Thompson, was born.

His many years in the army's ordnance department gave John Thompson a thorough knowledge of the U.S. weapons arsenal—and also of potential gun developers. In 1916, Thompson sent a telegram to a man named Theodore Eickhoff, inviting him to come to Pennsylvania to talk about a job opportunity. Eickhoff had joined the army just out of college and had initially worked under Thompson in the ordnance deparment.

John Thompson at West Point

Just thirty years old, Eickhoff had left the military the year before and now was helping out with his family's apple-cider mill. He arrived in his best suit and a stiff hat, his finest manners in tow, because meeting with a colonel was an "unusual and great experience." But the interview almost started out badly. On the ride from the train station, Thompson told him about the rifle-manufacturing plant he was running and how "particularly elated" he was that barrel production had climbed to 200 per day. All Eickhoff could think of, however, were wooden barrels meant for cider. After listening to the colonel for a few minutes, Eickhoff started to inquire what he was doing with all those empty barrels.

Then he realized his confusion. "Why you dumbbell, wake up!" he said to himself. "He is manufacturing rifles, and obviously is talking about 'rifle barrels.'"

On the ride, Thompson confided in Eickhoff that he was raising money to build an automatic rifle. He asked Eickhoff to be his chief engineer.

Though he didn't have a background in gun design, Eickhoff accepted and moved into a spare room in the Thompson house to begin work.

Around the world, others were also trying to make a powerful automatic rifle, with mixed success. The French government, seeing the same military need as Colonel Thompson for "walking fire"—quick-firing weapons carried by individual soldiers—adopted the Chauchat, a cheaply made rifle that came with a folding bipod attached for shooting from a prone position. Called "show-show" by American troops, it was truly automatic, emptying its twenty bullets with one pull of the trigger. But heavy parts in the gun moved back and forth with every shot, causing it to jerk violently. It weighed about twenty pounds and

A soldier uses a Chauchat in army maneuvers in 1918.

was notoriously unreliable; parts were badly made and broke easily, and ammunition got stuck in the half-moon-shaped magazine. In addition, its size and weight required two soldiers, one to carry the gun and another to carry the ammunition.

Still, thousands of Chauchat guns would be issued to American soldiers. Said U.S. Marine Corps machine-gun expert George Chinn: "No more crudely designed nor uglier automatic weapon has ever been put in the hands of soldiers of a first-rate power than this weapon."

Recognizing the need for an automatic weapon as the war in Europe progressed, the American gun designer John Moses Browning began work on his own version. Browning had made his first gun as a teenager and was something of a gun genius. Setting up shop in Ogden, Utah, he designed dozens of different weapons for the military during his lifetime, including the Colt .45 automatic pistol, machine guns, and rifles. By 1917, Browning had developed the Browning Automatic Rifle, which could fire twenty shots in two-and-a-half seconds.

The weapon, which came to be known by its initials, BAR, weighed more than seventeen pounds loaded and could be awkward to handle. When shot from the shoulder, the gun and its rapid recoil could knock the shooter off balance, sending the muzzle to the right, or up in the air, or both. This was a particular problem for those standing to the right when an inexperienced soldier began to shoot. "Some near tragedies were narrowly avoided," noted one reviewer.

John Moses Browning (left) and a rifle expert examine a Browning Automatic Rifle.

John Thompson imagined a gun that was lighter in weight and far simpler to shoot than the BAR or Chauchat. He sought to reduce the recoil and potential for mishaps by using a "blowback" mechanism, which uses the force of the spent bullet cartridge to reload the chamber. As ammunition is forced through the barrel, gas pressure separates the bullet from its casing, sending the bullet forward but the casing backward. There it can drive the bolt open and compress a spring, allowing the casing to be ejected. As the bolt closes, a new cartridge slips into the chamber.

This method used fewer moving parts, but it didn't work well with high-powered rifle ammunition, which could hit the bolt when pressure was still high, creating the possibility of an unexpected explosion. Thompson studied patents and found a design by John Blish, a career U.S. Navy officer. Blish believed that a metal wedge incorporated into the mechanism would act as something of a temporary lock, holding the bolt closed just a smidgen longer so that pressure could fall a bit before the casing was ejected and a new cartridge was loaded. Thus the gun would shoot, eject a cartridge, and load again rapidly, smoothly, and safely.

Under Thompson's direction, Eickhoff began to work on an automatic rifle using a machine shop in Cleveland, Ohio, to make parts. In February 1917, Eickhoff relocated to Cleveland and set up an office, hiring some staff.

When the United States joined the world war in April 1917, Thompson was called back into the army to help get rifles and other arms manufactured and off to U.S. soldiers. The need for a lightweight automatic weapon had become much clearer. The trench warfare in Europe was brutal, and fighting it required significant firepower. The

Germans had come to the war with thousands of machine guns, but the British and Americans had started out with only a few hundred. John Browning's BAR was ready to go, and the U.S. military adopted it.

Meanwhile, Eickhoff's gun wasn't working well at all. The metal parts jammed and the rifle ammunition got stuck in the chamber. When a prototype of the rifle was tested in August 1917, part of the mechanism exploded.

In experimenting, Eickhoff realized that rifle ammunition just wouldn't work properly in the mechanism unless every cartridge was waxed or oiled. However, the shorter, fatter, slower .45-caliber

cartridges—the same ones John Thompson had recommended for army pistols—worked perfectly every time. Though effective at relatively short distances, they couldn't offer the long-range accuracy expected from a rifle. Eickhoff realized that the outlook for a new automatic rifle was bleak.

In September 1917, Eickhoff traveled to Washington to share the bad news. Thompson listened carefully from behind his big desk. Rather than being angry or upset about the gun's shortcomings, he immediately saw different possibilities for a rapid-firing weapon that filled a gap between the short range of a pistol and the long range of a rifle. The Chauchat and the BAR were too heavy and awkward for the war that was being fought, Thompson told him. The soldiers in the trenches, he said, "need a small machine gun, a gun that will fire fifty to one hundred rounds, so light that a man can drag it with him as he crawls on his belly from trench to trench and wipe out a whole company single-handed."

So, Thompson told Eickhoff, that's what they would make. It would be "a one-man, handheld machine gun. A trench broom."

A gun to sweep away the enemy.

And then, to demonstrate, Thompson stood up and pretended to fire this powerful new gun from his hip, spraying the room with imaginary rounds. An entirely new kind of weapon was on its way.

Theodore Eickhoff gives an early prototype a workout.

CHAPTER 3
THE ANNIHILATOR

WITHIN DAYS OF THOMPSON'S REQUEST for a trench broom, a new gun was on the drawing board in Cleveland. In truth, it looked more like a toy than an enemy destroyer. It had two grips, one for each hand, and a cartoonish, deeply grooved barrel.

The team nicknamed it the "Persuader."

Leading the design effort was a twenty-three-year-old prodigy named Oscar V. Payne, who had started working as a draftsman at sixteen. Payne, a natural artist without any formal training, had learned guns inside and out working for patent lawyers whose clients included several large gunmakers. That work called for him to draw detailed images for patent applications and pictures for use in lawsuits.

When the war began, his firm's business dropped off and Payne prepared to join the fighting in Europe. A boss suggested he see first if his services might be useful to the army's ordnance department. He was directed to now-Brigadier General John Thompson. Holding his

24

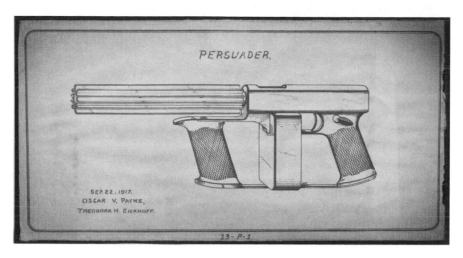

The first design for a "trench broom," nicknamed the "Persuader"

hat in his hand, Payne introduced himself and asked for advice about joining the armed forces.

To Payne's surprise, Thompson recognized his name. "I know all about you," Thompson told him. "Don't enlist." Instead, he encouraged the young man to sit tight, saying, "I have something in mind where you can use your talent and be of great service to your country." Within a few weeks, Payne was hired to work in Cleveland for $150 a month, equal to a modest annual salary today of about $33,000.

The urgent wartime work in Cleveland was done in complete secrecy. Theodore Eickhoff was told to purchase equipment in his own name and never mention the company he worked for or the project. The team worked in a two-story frame house on Euclid Avenue, near a stretch once known as Millionaire's Row for its dozens of grand and stately mansions. On the second floor, a growing group of men worked on design and mechanics. Stuffing cotton into their ears, they tested firing mechanisms by shooting ammunition into a large, padded pipe as the room filled with smoke. The pipe ran twelve feet, through the carpentry

On Euclid Avenue, gun mechanisms were tested by firing bullets through a long pipe into a reinforced, sand-filled box in the next room.

shop, into another room. There the bullets sprayed into a four-by-four-foot box filled with sand and steel plates, where the ammunition was reduced to "jumbled bits of lead and steel."

Behind the secretive Cleveland team was a real company backed by unusually deep pockets. In the summer of 1916, around the time he contacted Eickhoff, John Thompson had formed Auto-Ordnance Corporation, with headquarters in New York. Thompson and his wife, Juliet, were owners. Commander Blish was given a piece of the company in exchange for using his patents. But the real money to support it largely came from a family connection.

In August 1914, John Thompson's son Marcellus H. Thompson had married Dorothy Harvey in an elaborate wedding where a full orchestra entertained 500 guests. Marcellus's new father-in-law was the editor and power broker George Harvey, who had been a reporter and then managing editor of the *New York World* as a very young man. Seeking to make more money, Harvey moved into the business world, coming in contact with the aggressive financier Thomas Fortune Ryan, who had wrangled the contracts to build New York's streetcar and elevated rail systems. In the 1890s, Harvey won the rights to build similar public transit systems on Staten Island and in New Jersey, and then in Havana, Cuba, making a bundle.

George Harvey,
around 1914

Thomas Fortune Ryan, around 1910

With his proceeds, Harvey bought the prestigious magazine *North American Review*. He later became president of Harper & Brothers, a book publisher and owner of *Harper's Weekly*. Now in his fifties, he, too, became an owner in Auto-Ordnance.

The aptly named Thomas Fortune Ryan was a former banker and stockbroker who was considered a ruthless businessman. After making millions of dollars on New York's early transit system, he went on to control part of the U.S. tobacco industry. He made *Forbes* magazine's first list of America's richest men, with wealth estimated at about $70 million.

A big man, described as six feet, two inches tall, and a devout Catholic, he rarely gave interviews or took a public stance. The *New York Times* called him "the Sphinx of Wall Street" after Ryan told an interviewer, "I am afraid that I am not much of a talker." A longtime business partner once called him "the most adroit, suave, and noiseless man that American finance has ever known."

At least partly as a favor to his old friend George Harvey, Ryan provided the money to allow Thompson to develop his powerful weapon. Though it wasn't a large amount for a man of Ryan's wealth, the funding was plentiful for the start-up business. Over and over after the United States entered the war, Thompson urged his developers to hurry up—and not to worry about cost. Eickhoff submitted expenses to Ryan's office manager each month and was paid directly by Ryan's office.

While Eickhoff and Payne were under pressure to produce a working gun in Cleveland, Thompson was similarly under the gun in his military job in the ordnance department. American soldiers needed reliable rifles. But Thompson thought the British's Enfield rifles were out of date. The ammunition they used wasn't easily available in the United States and sometimes jammed. To the surprise of many, he rejected those rifles as inadequate for American soldiers.

Almost single-handedly, Thompson held up U.S. rifle production for four months while the rifle was retooled to have more interchangeable parts and to use American-made ammunition.

His superiors backed him, but he came under intense criticism from some congressmen for his stubbornness. Senator George E. Chamberlain, the chair of the Military Affairs Committee, lambasted the ordnance department, saying that "while the house was burning," it spent months fiddling with the rifle and ammunition.

Following pages: Auto-Ordnance employees at work in the engineering drafting room

Ultimately, the effort paid off. The new version was more reliable, and American factories turned out thousands of the .30-caliber, Model 1917 United States rifle daily, providing American fighters overseas with more than one million firearms.

Thompson later was awarded the Distinguished Service Medal for his work. In an article published in multiple newspapers, an admiring writer compared him to Henry Ford, who had standardized manufacturing for the new automobiles that were replacing horses and taking the country by storm. Thompson, the writer gushed, is "America's premier gunman."

During an interview at Thompson's Washington home, with photos of his father and son nearby, the white-haired military man puffed on a cigar as he spelled out his management philosophy. "My principle has been to select big, broad, and efficient men, and put them to work at something they know how to do," he said. "Say to them: There's your job. Go to it. Go to it in your own way. Stand on your head if you want to in getting it done, but get it done!"

Still, even while giving his people support, he said, "don't lie down in a furrow and go to sleep," but pay attention to the details and "follow the work up."

Thompson followed his own advice with his fledgling company. He was in regular contact through the mail and, increasingly, through visits to Cleveland. Often he took a prototype to a firing range to try it out. Though he wanted the gun developed quickly, he also pushed for better parts and better reliability, sending his team back again and again for improvements. Eickhoff remembered Thompson as a kind and thoughtful leader, though also incredibly demanding and precise. "If you did something he didn't like, he could surely take you to task for it," he said. "He could give you a mental pinch." Though Thompson repeatedly said cost wasn't an issue, he paid attention when Eickhoff spent money that Thompson thought was unnecessary; then, the older man might offer a lesson on the appropriate use of OPM, or "other people's money."

While the Persuader looked slick on paper, the actual prototypes were disappointing. To keep the gun lightweight, Eickhoff and Payne chose the lightest components available. Instead of the magazine included in the initial drawing, they tried to feed in ammunition from a belt, which could be loaded at a factory rather than in the field. But a belt full of cartridges was heavy, and the prototype gun jammed over and over, never firing more than seven bullets at a time.

Eickhoff (far left) and Payne (far right) join the Auto-Ordnance staff for a picnic around 1918.

Eventually, Eickhoff and Payne realized the belt wouldn't work. So they started over, using sturdier materials and a twenty-cartridge rectangular magazine like the one used by the Colt pistol.

They nicknamed this version the "Annihilator."

Finally, in the summer of 1918, the pieces began to come together. The gun was working exactly as envisioned, releasing a barrage of fire that drained the magazine in the blink of an eye. Once the mechanism was in place, the team focused on making it more durable and perfecting its external features. They spent the fall working long hours to make samples that might be tested in battle.

But while the gun was coming together in Cleveland, the war was coming to an end in Europe.

By November 11, 1918—Armistice Day—Auto-Ordnance finally had a gun ready. As the reports came in that Germany and the Allies had signed a cease-fire agreement on the Western Front, the hardworking team in Cleveland wrestled with the news. They were joyous that the war was over—but they also knew the harsh reality ahead.

Oscar Payne looked at Eickhoff and summed it up: "It looks like we missed the boat."

CHAPTER 4
READY ... AIM

EVEN THOUGH THE WAR WAS OVER, Thompson
and Auto-Ordnance remained optimistic. Both politicians and military
men were arguing that the nation should be better prepared for war in
the future. In addition to the troubles providing adequate rifles, the
U.S. military was the only force without a serious commitment to
lightweight, handheld, automatic guns, which left American soldiers at
a disadvantage.

The Italians had fought with the Revelli, a twin-barreled automatic
pistol that was usually fired from a fixed mount. In response, the Germans introduced the Bergmann machine pistol in mid-1918, an impressive automatic weapon that was similar in concept to Thompson's gun.
Happily for the Americans, only a few thousand reached the front lines.
But the enemy's use of such firearms increased Thompson's hope that
the United States might want a similar weapon.

Thompson was formally discharged from the army in December

1918 and pressed forward to get his gun into production. He also began to look for other outlets beyond the military, seeing a potential market for police and foreign armies.

By spring 1919, Auto-Ordnance had a staff of about twenty-five in a new office in Cleveland putting together prototypes for demonstration, drafting specifications, and working on improvements. During this time, Payne also developed an unusual new magazine, a round drum that could hold fifty or one hundred cartridges, more than any other handheld gun. Grooves and a central clock-type spring inside the drum pushed the bullets upward through a spiraling path, one by one, into the firing mechanism. "The raising of 100 cartridges against gravity," *Army and Navy Journal* said, "is a remarkable and hitherto unaccomplished feat." The round magazine, along with the weapon's two grips, gave the gun a unique profile, making it almost instantly recognizable.

Inside the Thompson's drum magazine, springlike mechanisms move fifty or one hundred bullets through the grooves and up into the gun.

Now, said Eickhoff, "the time was ripe to give the child an official name." Thompson balked at calling it a machine gun because machine guns traditionally were heavier and fired rifle cartridges. They considered "machine pistol" and "autogun," but settled on "submachine gun" to describe a handheld automatic weapon firing pistol cartridges.

At the Auto-Ordnance annual meeting, surrounded by antiques in Thomas Fortune Ryan's opulent New York office, Thompson suggested the gun be named after its chief financial backer. But Ryan wanted nothing of it. "I'm no military man and what is more, I know nothing about guns," he said.

Thompson also suggested naming it after its main designer, Payne, but that, too, was shot down. To Ryan and the rest of the group, the decision was simple: The gun should carry the name of the esteemed military man who conceived it. So, it was christened the Thompson submachine gun.

While the staff put the finishing touches on the Thompson gun, other Auto-Ordnance employees returned to trying to build additional weapons, though none would ever make it to market.

At the end of 1919, Marcellus Thompson, who had fought well in several battles in Europe, resigned from the army and joined the company to help with marketing and promotion.

In 1920, the Thompsons and their team set to work introducing their baby to the world—and finding a good home for it. In April, the U.S. Army tested a stripped-down prototype of the gun, capable of firing up to 1,500 rounds a minute (if you could cram that much ammunition in) and reported that it didn't overheat or jam. The Marines gave the gun a similar run-through in the summer.

In August, the company demonstrated the gun at the National Rifle Matches at Camp Perry, Ohio, which were run by the National Rifle Association. When an Auto-Ordnance employee put the gun to his hip and pulled the trigger, "a sheet of flame" burst from the muzzle. Shiny spent cartridges showered from the breech. Shots tore through the air in "one long roar." Not surprisingly, crowds gathered to see the dazzling new weapon in its public debut.

In September, the New York Police Department made news when it ordered ten of the groundbreaking guns. It said it would use them for controlling riots and chasing bandits, who were outrunning the police with faster automobiles coming off the lines in Detroit. Prohibition had begun in January, after the ratification of the Eighteenth Amendment to the U.S. Constitution, which banned the sale and manufacture of liquor, beer, and wine. Rather than encouraging citizens to stop drinking, the new law began to drive otherwise honest people to seek out illegal booze. Over time, networks of gangsters began to bubble up to provide liquor and beer to the thirsty. The explosion in illegal bootlegging and rum-running would eventually challenge local police—and provide some unexpected business for Auto-Ordnance.

As the nation began to adapt to Prohibition, Auto-Ordnance officials traveled around the country to demonstrate the gun to law enforcement and drum up orders. They touted their weapon as powerful but lightweight, and small enough to tuck comfortably under a coat.

Police forces in Cleveland, Boston, Philadelphia, and Los Angeles, among other cities, took a look. Under a headline, "Might Help in Kansas City," the local paper noted, "With it, it is claimed, an inexperienced marksman can do efficient work on moving targets by using

John and Marcellus Thompson in late 1920

An Auto-Ordnance publicity photo shows two New York City policemen
demonstrating an Annihilator prototype.

the gun as a fireman uses a hose." The Portland, Oregon, police attended a demonstration of a weapon that, one writer said, "is guaranteed to put lead and the fear of God into the heart of the fastest fading criminal."

Los Angeles ordered one gun, which prompted the police chief to promise that criminals who broke into houses or held people up "are going to have about 99 per cent less chance of escaping from the clutches of the law in the future."

While others showed off the gun to potential buyers across the United States, John Thompson began talking with the Colt's Patent Fire Arms Manufacturing Company about mass-producing it. The large gunmaker looked carefully at it, and made a surprising offer: It would buy all the rights for $1 million, twice what had been invested so far.

Thomas Fortune Ryan, who knew something about making money, saw the offer as a good omen and turned it down. He told Thompson, "If it's worth a million to them, it's worth more than a million to us."

Instead, Auto-Ordnance ordered a whopping 15,000 guns from Colt's. These would be a bit heavier than the demonstration models, between eight and nine pounds. They would fire at a rate of something less than 1,000 rounds a minute and include a lever to switch from automatic to semiautomatic, which required that the trigger be pulled for each bullet. The guns would be elegantly made, with blued steel and a removable butt stock made of handsome walnut.

Once the order was placed with Colt's in 1920, the Auto-Ordnance team in Cleveland was dismantled. Most of that staff was let go, except for Eickhoff and Payne, who moved to Hartford, Connecticut, to join the

Following pages: In 1922, Auto-Ordnance demonstrated a Thompson "anti-bandit gun" mounted on a motorcycle sidecar, which was also equipped with an experimental wireless radio receiver.

Thompsons. The remaining company was little more than a sales and marketing office in New York City, but there was plenty of selling and marketing to do to move that many guns. The company cranked up the publicity and began to look for new uses for what *Scientific American* called a "pocket machine gun" that was "probably the most efficient man-killer of any firearm yet produced."

When the first guns rolled off Colt's manufacturing line at the end of March 1921, a few were sent off to the U.S. Army and Marines, which ran them through more tests. Though the military officials lauded the guns for "nearly mechanical perfection" and reliability, they didn't see much application for them. Since they weren't rifles, the guns weren't very accurate at long ranges, so the Marines concluded they might be useful for artillery, away from the front lines. The testing board said they might also be used for lookout duty, to protect supply trains, or for warfare in the jungle.

The gun would be tested again in 1922. But it was neither a rifle nor a pistol nor a traditional machine gun, and the military just didn't know what to do with it.

The company even tried to sell the idea of an attack from the skies. It floated the idea of rigging up thirty Thompson submachine guns on an open-cockpit, low-wing airplane, which then could literally rain fire (and empty casings) down below.

Still, no U.S. military orders were placed.

John Thompson had envisioned his weapon for war, and his team had worked hard to make it useful for American soldiers. But the "War to End All Wars" was over, and he would have to find other buyers instead.

With a gun, a stock, and a one-hundred-shot magazine selling for $225—about half the cost of a car at the time—the company ratcheted up its marketing to policemen and sheriffs. Auto-Ordnance also suggested that guards in banks and companies facing labor protests or strikes might also find it useful. For riot control, it even offered a special cartridge with birdshot, which theoretically would be less damaging than regular .45-caliber bullets, so the situation could "be handled by officers of the law in the most humane manner possible." Unfortunately, the shot scattered in an unpredictable way; one tester who aimed those bullets at a target said that none of the birdshot could be found after firing.

In May 1922, the company put on an elaborate demonstration for police in New York and New Jersey with all the drama of a Hollywood production.

A police officer with a Thompson gun mounted on his motorcycle took aim at a moving car full of dummy gangsters, first shredding the tires. Two more officers joined him, and the trio opened fire on the car itself. The back "was perforated til it looked like a Swiss cheese, the radiator was torn to shreds, the gas tank resembled a nutmeg-grater, and the steering gear was turned into an indescribable mass of kindling wood and twisted metal," one reporter wrote. Then, for good measure, a bullet was fired into the spilled gasoline. The whole thing whooshed into a ball of fire.

The shooters "converted a solid-looking seven-passenger touring car into a flaming mass of junk in less than a minute," wrote another observer. "Nothing in the machine larger than a mouse could have survived the fusillade."

It was an impressive and memorable demonstration. But sales still languished.

The Thompson Submachine Gun
The Most Effective Portable Fire Arm In Existence

THE ideal weapon for the protection of large estates, ranches, plantations, etc. A combination machine gun and semi-automatic shoulder rifle in the form of a pistol. A compact, tremendously powerful, yet simply operated machine gun weighing only seven pounds and having only *thirty* parts. Full automatic, fired from the hip, 1,500 shots per minute. Semi-automatic, fitted with a stock and fired from the shoulder, 50 shots per minute. Magazines hold 50 and 100 cartridges.

THE Thompson Submachine Gun incorporates the simplicity and infallibility of a hand loaded weapon with the effectiveness of a machine gun. It is simple, safe, sturdy, and sure in action. In addition to its increasingly wide use for protection purposes by banks, industrial plants, railroads, mines, ranches, plantations, etc., it has been adopted by leading Police and Constabulary Forces, throughout the world and is unsurpassed for military purposes.

Information and prices promptly supplied on request

AUTO-ORDNANCE CORPORATION
302 Broadway   *Cable address: Autordco*   New York City

An Auto-Ordnance ad from the early 1920s

46

The guns were also sent to hardware and sporting-goods dealers to be sold in their communities. *Hardware Dealers' Magazine* featured the Thompson in 1921 in a long list of "the latest money-making things" stores could offer, sandwiched between a crib that could be used in a car and an electric egg beater. It said the gun "is described as an ideal weapon for the protection of large estates, ranches, plantations, etc." Soon after, Auto-Ordnance began running ads promoting the gun for sportsmen and those who wanted to protect their property from invaders.

Auto-Ordnance made another, particularly astonishing proposal: A Thompson submachine gun, spitting dozens of bullets in seconds, could offer a homeowner protection from burglars. "So it came to pass," wrote William J. Helmer, a biographer of the gun, "that the Thompson—manufactured in peacetime, sold on the commercial market—was, in a sense, a machine gun for the home."

Even before the gun was mass-produced, Auto-Ordnance sales flyers had also begun to sport a new slogan: "On the Side of Law and Order."

At least, that was John Thompson's intention.

CHAPTER 5
REBELLION

JUST WEEKS AFTER THE FIRST GUNS started rolling off Colt's manufacturing line, the new weapon was already embroiled in controversy.

On a Sunday in June 1921, William McNarney was helping to prepare the steamship *East Side* for a trip to Ireland. The ship was scheduled to leave Hoboken, New Jersey, shortly. It was to stop in Norfolk, Virginia, for a load of coal and then head to Dublin. As the chief steward, McNarney was responsible for meals on the ship as well as keeping track of supplies.

That afternoon, he went down to the icebox and was surprised to find burlap bags piled up in an alleyway nearby.

Because the bags were in his way, he reached down to see what was in them and was shocked to recognize the butt of a gun. Curious, he found a knife and slashed open a bag. It was filled with guns. Concerned about violence on the upcoming trip, he reported his find to his superiors.

A U.S. official stands beside the nearly 500 guns seized from a ship bound for Ireland in June 1921.

On June 15, U.S. Customs officials swarmed the ship. By then, the guns had been hidden, and it took three searches to find the stash. But what a stash it was: four hundred ninety-five brand-new Thompson submachine guns, plus dozens of boxes of magazines and spare parts—all apparently bound for nationalist fighters in Ireland.

The accidental discovery sparked a gunrunning scandal that threatened the friendship between the United States and Great Britain, the reputation of the Thompson submachine gun, and even relationships within John Thompson's family.

For centuries, Ireland had been under British rule. On Easter Monday 1916, while the world war raged in Germany, a group of Irish nationals had occupied key buildings in Dublin and proclaimed the creation of an independent Irish Republic.

The British crushed the rebellion in a week. But the influence of the Easter Rising grew, along with the desire for independence. In January 1919, a small, determined group began the Anglo-Irish War, or the Irish War of Independence.

This war was nothing like the one that had just been fought in Europe. The group, which became known as the Irish Republican Army, was short of money, men, and arms. So it fought a new kind of war, a guerrilla war, in which volunteers launched surprise attacks on government property, British police, and soldiers. The rebels then slipped back into their daily lives, disappearing from view.

In fact, just a day after U.S. officials found those guns on that ship in Hoboken, the Thompson guns got a tryout in Dublin—unknown to anyone in America.

At 8:30 in the morning on June 16, 1921, a group of Irish rebels staked out a train carrying about 300 British troops near Drumcondra, just north of Dublin. As the train passed by, the rebels threw grenades. A fighter named Charles Dalton aimed a Thompson submachine gun, but couldn't figure out how to fire it before the train passed by. Another man with a Thompson successfully emptied a full magazine of fifty bullets into a car.

The attack happened so quickly that the British soldiers didn't have a chance to fire back. The explosions were great enough that bricks on nearby houses were chipped, and a group of boys on their way to school hurriedly sought safety in someone's home. Windows in the train were blown out, and one train car was riddled with bullets. Three British soldiers were injured, one seriously, though no rebels were hurt.

How did a brand-new automatic weapon find its way to Ireland? The answer is a bit of a lesson in supply and demand. Auto-Ordnance needed customers—and the Irish guerrillas needed effective weapons.

In late 1920, violence had escalated in the Irish War of Independence. Around that time, Michael Collins, a key leader of the revolt, clipped an article about the Thompson gun from the November 1920 issue of *Popular Mechanics* and asked an aide to look into it.

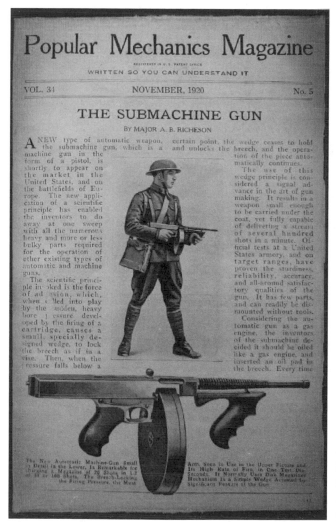

Sinn Fein leader Michael Collins saw this article in *Popular Mechanics* and was intrigued.

In the United States, middlemen were helping Irish supporters get an audience at Auto-Ordnance. That likely had something to do with the company's financier, Thomas Fortune Ryan. Born to Irish immigrant parents, Ryan had once belonged to an Irish nationalist group and was friendly with Irish Republican leaders in America and Ireland. He had the connections to make sales—and the interest in helping.

But if Ryan was involved in getting guns to Ireland, his work was invisible. Instead, the job fell to Marcellus Thompson and Auto-Ordnance's secretary-treasurer, Frank Merkling. The younger Thompson was trying to find buyers in the United States and abroad, including Latin America and Great Britain. In December 1920, the company approached British officials about buying the weapons but didn't land a commitment. In early 1921, Marcellus asked a salesman to "see what the Irish crowd thought about the gun."

Between January and May, several buyers, all apparently using fictitious names, managed to place orders for hundreds of Thompson guns. Apart from the guns discovered on the SS *East Side,* more than eighty guns were thought to have made their way to Irish rebels.

One cache of about thirty guns, believed to be early prototypes, was hidden in a sofa and two overstuffed chairs on a ship and then unloaded in Cork in April 1921. A batch of about fifty new guns arrived via another ship in July.

James Dineen and Patrick Cronin, two Irish-American men who were U.S. Army officers during World War I, each smuggled a gun into Ireland in his suitcase. They arrived in the spring to show Irish fighters how the gun worked and how to care for it, and they put on showy demonstrations. In one, Cronin took aim at a tin can. After his first shot lifted it into the air, he continued to hit the can in midair again and again.

An Auto-Ordnance employee demonstrates the gun for British officers in 1921.

In May 1921, Dineen and Cronin met Michael Collins and other IRA leaders in the basement of an empty suburban home. They urged Collins to try the gun out by taking aim at bricks placed against the wall, but Collins declined.

Tom Barry, leader of the Cork No. 3 Brigade, was offered the chance next. He, too, tried to say no. Writing about the experience later, he said he worried that "I would miss with this new-fangled gun." Then he was certain the rest of the group "would rag me unmercifully and probably offer to teach me to shoot." Finally, he took the weapon "and with great luck smashed all the bricks into smithereens."

The IRA leaders were so impressed that they were eager to receive the nearly 500 guns that were supposed to be coming soon from the States.

On board the *East Side,* an Irish engineering crew, taking advantage of a strike, had offered their services to the captain. Once hired, they were able to load bags and boxes of guns and parts on board, saying they were engineering supplies. They might have gotten away with the smuggling if they had been somewhat less sloppy about where they left the loot.

Once the guns were detected, the new engineering team disappeared—and it became clear the guns weren't going to be arriving in Ireland anytime soon.

A man who said his name was Frank Williams then tried to get the Thompson guns back. Shortly after federal customs agents seized the guns, Williams told the Hoboken police that he had purchased 600 new Thompson submachine guns and had hired a truck driver to move them—but, he said, the truck driver had stolen them instead. Williams wanted the Hoboken police to take possession of the guns.

What followed, said the *New York Times,* was "a day replete with mystery, rumor, denials, and counter-denials." For a time, the Hoboken police were able to take control of the guns from federal Customs officials, and both guarded the weapons the first night.

While the two sides haggled, a crowd of newspaper reporters crammed into the Hoboken police station. Some noted that Frank Williams had a "pronounced Irish accent." But when they asked his attorney about the brogue, he tried to correct them. "Surely you mean a Canadian accent," the lawyer responded.

Finally, a federal judge insisted the Hoboken police turn over the guns to the feds, who whisked them away to a warehouse.

How had so many guns become available? And how had a mysterious man like Frank Williams been able to buy 600 guns? John

Thompson, who was in Europe, didn't offer any insight. "For the present I shall say nothing," he said.

Marcellus Thompson said it was a mystery to him.

It wasn't such a mystery to the British, however. The British government had invited John Thompson to visit London to talk about the guns. But while Thompson was in London in May, British forces in Ireland captured a document from the IRA that spelled out how a large order of Thompson submachine guns would be spread around the country in the fight for independence.

Marcellus Thompson crafted a letter of response to the British Consul in early June, less than two weeks before the *East Side* incident, proclaiming innocence. "To begin with," he wrote, "the Auto-Ordnance Corporation is a company in too high a standing to countenance any underhanded dealings in the gun business with those operating against the constituted authorities." He continued, "Our advertisements as well as our policy distinctly enunciate the principle 'On the Side of Law and Order.'"

He went on to say that the company was producing only fifteen to twenty guns a day. "I can assure you," he wrote, it had no large orders in the United States so far. Most foreign orders came from foreign governments, rather than individuals.

"We realize that this gun is a very dangerous weapon indeed; in fact, it is the most effective portable firearm in existence," he said. "We are correspondingly careful of the responsibility that rests upon our shoulders."

Company documents uncovered during the investigation, however, told another story. Frank Williams, partly through an intermediary, had, in fact, ordered 600 guns. As firearms came off Colt's production line, hundreds of them had been delivered to Williams, and fifty more were delivered to a different man, who was also likely shipping them to Ireland.

In much smaller quantities, just-manufactured Thompson guns were going around the world to foreign governments interested in military uses or keeping citizens in line. One or more guns went to Panama, El Salvador, Cuba, Costa Rica, Colombia, Honduras, Bolivia, Greece, Spain, and even England. They also were being shipped all over the United States, to Boston, Detroit, St. Louis, and towns as small as Live Oak, Florida, and Bismarck, North Dakota. But the mysterious Williams and the other buyer were, without a doubt, Auto-Ordnance's best customers.

At the U.S. Justice Department, the key point person investigating the *East Side* was a young man from the Bureau of Investigation named J. Edgar Hoover. Called Edgar by his mother, he also sometimes went

A young J. Edgar Hoover helped investigate the *East Side* gunrunning scandal and became director of the Bureau of Investigation three years later.

by J.E. But his friends at school nicknamed him "Speed" for the rapid-fire, almost machine-gun-like way he talked, a mannerism he had adopted to overcome a childhood stuttering problem.

A onetime file clerk who attended law school at night, the twenty-six-year-old Hoover was ambitious and driven. Government documents show that he oversaw each interview and assigned men to dig into the backgrounds of some of the buyers as well as Merkling, the Auto-Ordnance secretary-treasurer. He also asked Bureau men to "shadow" them and report back on where they went, when, and what they did. They didn't find much, but they built an impressive file.

Just three years later, at the age of twenty-nine, Hoover would become director of the Bureau of Investigation, which specialized in analyzing information, collecting evidence, and interviewing witnesses. The *East Side* case would be Hoover's first introduction to the Thompson submachine gun. In the 1930s, the gun would help reshape his agency and change the course of his career.

On July 8, 1921, the Irish rebels used their weapons again at the Bally-fermot Bridge, about four miles from Dublin. Nationalist guerrillas dropped gasoline on a passing train with both regular citizens and troops on board, while a fighter opened fire with a Thompson gun. The civilians scrambled to duck under their seats. Several civilians were injured and one was killed.

Before the Thompson gun could be used again, the IRA and British reached a truce on July 11. Most counties in Ireland would become part of a free state that would govern itself. But the country would remain part of the British Empire. The truce ended the fighting with Great Britain, but it led to a two-year civil war between those who agreed with the treaty and those who wanted a permanent and complete separation.

Meanwhile, in the United States, a government investigation plodded forward. In June 1922, a whole year after the guns were found, the government announced it had indicted Marcellus Thompson, Merkling, and several others, along with Auto-Ordnance itself, charging them with shipping guns to rebels to fight the United Kingdom, a friend of the United States. The alleged crime carried a penalty of up to three years in jail.

Being accused of a serious crime was embarrassing to the company, which feared the news would further hurt sales. And it was especially embarrassing to Marcellus Thompson. His father-in-law, George Harvey, had helped engineer Warren Harding's nomination for president. With Harding now president, Harvey was serving as ambassador to Great Britain. The news that his son-in-law may have sold arms to a British enemy was awkward at best. Harvey chose not to discuss it in public.

Marcellus Thompson insisted he was innocent, saying, "Of course, we would not think of selling guns to persons we might even suspect of reselling them into the hands of enemies of constituted governments."

Ultimately, the U.S. government decided it didn't have much of a case. Great Britain had reached an agreement with Ireland and it lost interest in pushing for prosecution. In addition, U.S. law had changed at the end of World War I, and the government belatedly decided that selling guns to Irish rebels was legal after all.

In early 1923, the government dropped the charges.

In a promotional photo, Dorothy Harvey Thompson posed with a Thompson—an image that didn't play very well after guns heading to Ireland were confiscated.

Still, the incident caused a painful rift between the Thompson and Harvey families that never fully healed. In 1923, Dorothy Harvey went to visit her parents in London and stayed even after her father left his position and returned to the United States. Sometime after, she and Marcellus separated, and they formally divorced in 1929.

Despite the *East Side* debacle, many Thompson submachine guns made their way into Ireland. An additional sixty guns were secretly delivered to Frank Williams just weeks after the *East Side* guns were discovered. During the Irish Civil War from 1921 to 1923, the British-backed Free State forces purchased and used the guns as well.

In 1925, a representative of Frank Williams won the seized guns back from the U.S. government. Most were in a government warehouse, but a

A general for provisional government troops in Ireland carries a Thompson gun during the Irish Civil War.

few had to be retrieved from the Department of Justice, Customs, and the U.S. Attorney's office in Newark, New Jersey.

Underscoring the way powerful weapons can make their way around the world, many of those returned Thompson guns are believed to have ultimately made their way to Ireland after all—including some that may have been smuggled in by an Irish soccer team that toured America in 1927, in part to raise funds for the IRA.

All in all, Auto-Ordnance escaped without too much damage. Its guns finally had been tested in war—though not a traditional one. But it still had another, equally uncomfortable problem: Guns that came off the production line were stacking up for lack of buyers. The company had to build temporary racks to store them.

In 1922, Oscar Payne left the company for another job, after earning twenty-four patents related to his designs. In 1924, Theodore Eickhoff, whose hearing was permanently damaged by his work developing the gun, looked carefully at the situation and decided to take another job. "The future of the gun business did not look bright," Eickhoff said.

Nor did the future of John Thompson's creation.

CHAPTER 6

THE CHICAGO PIANO

IN THE EARLY FALL OF 1924, Dean O'Banion spent a pleasant month vacationing near Denver, Colorado, enjoying the outdoors and entertaining visitors. Often, the Chicago flower shop owner and bootlegger showed his guests the unusual perks of providing illegal beer and liquor to thirsty Chicago residents during Prohibition.

Taking visitors to his car, he would point out the half dozen bullet holes that dotted the back. "Got those in a fight with the Prohibition officers," he would say. "They didn't get me, though."

Then he would take them around to the front to show off a scar on the steering wheel. "Bullet," he said. "They got my driver."

The troubles didn't seem to bother him. "I'm a tough guy," he told his visitors. "You can bet your neck I'll keep a lot of breweries going till I get ready to quit."

Dean O'Banion and his wife, Viola

Near the end of his visit, he hosted a private rodeo for his new friends, put on by cowboys hired from miles around. He also made a special stop at a downtown Denver hardware dealer. There he picked up a few things to support his business: several rifles, a dozen or more revolvers, boxes of ammunition, and a new, lightweight machine gun.

Less than a month later, Dean O'Banion was dead. While he was arranging flowers for a funeral, three men entered his Chicago shop, greeted him, and gunned him down at close range.

°o° o

Under the surface, tension between the city's bootlegging gangs had been rolling to a boil as they battled to control lucrative territory to sell beer and liquor and run gambling houses. "The struggle for power in the underworld has embroiled virtually every gangster in the city," warned one newspaper.

The O'Banion murder was all but a declaration of war.

And in wars, those with the better weapons have the edge. The "machine gun" that O'Banion brought back in his bullet-pocked car was a Thompson—perhaps the first Thompson owned by gangsters there. Its fierce firepower promised victory to those who had it, and it would soon outrank the pistols and sawed-off shotguns that filled gangster arsenals, becoming the trademark weapon of Chicago's bad boys.

Dean O'Banion never tested his new gun. One rumor said he had once gone hunting for some west-side rivals with the submachine gun in hand, but it apparently was never fired.

Exactly when gangsters first used a Thompson gun isn't clear. In September 1925, a shooter who missed his target left a line of bullets near a drugstore, perplexing the police. One reporter guessed that a firing squad had lined up to take the shots.

Two weeks later, twenty of the same bullets showed up in a shooting that killed one man and injured another. This time, police concluded, "The bullets were fired by a machine gun."

With Prohibition going strong, gang shootings became almost a weekly ritual in Chicago. The use of the Thompson gun raised the ante—and the deaths. Police had nothing like it, nor did they have the cars or manpower to combat the increasingly wealthy and confident group of men who were supplying Chicago with illegal drinks.

In February 1926, more than a year after the gun first landed in Chicago, a Thompson shooting made the front pages—and suddenly everyone seemed to want one. Chicago police Captain John Stege declared that his force needed to be armed as well as the criminals and that he would ask permission to buy several.

Al Capone took notice, too. The gangster had a mean streak and unstoppable ambition to control his piece of Chicago's beer houses and gambling parlors. If there was a better weapon for taking care of his business, he wanted it.

Two Capone men visited a hardware dealer named Alex Korecek. One of them said he was a bank messenger in need of protection and easily bought a gun and a one-hundred-round magazine for $210.

Later, the pair went back to order two more. This time, Korecek doubted their story and tried to turn them away.

A Chicago police lieutenant tries out one of the department's new Thompson guns.

They clarified their request: Korecek could cooperate or be killed. The dealer sold them two more guns.

Not long after, a car full of men stopped at the Pony Inn in suburban Cicero for a boys' night out. As the men clambered from their car, shots burst forth before they even had a chance to turn around. In a matter of seconds, two men were dead and another was dying.

Two of the men were bootleggers. But the other was William Mc-Swiggin, a popular assistant state attorney who had earned the nickname "the hanging prosecutor."

An eyewitness reported seeing a "car speeding away with what looked like a telephone receiver sticking out of the rear window and spitting fire."

Chicago police Captain John Stege inspects hats and eyeglasses left behind after Assistant State Attorney William McSwiggin and two bootleggers were murdered.

Police and the press declared it a machine-gun murder. The *Chicago Daily Tribune* noted that the bullets "were of the copper-jacketed type used in the machine guns which of late have supplanted the less effective sawed-off shotgun as the favorite weapon of the gang killers."

Why McSwiggin was with the bootleggers wasn't clear. What mattered was that the murder crossed the line. An estimated 200 men had already died in the gang wars in the previous four years. But killing a public official was unacceptable.

Immediately, attention turned to Capone. (Later, police would accuse Capone himself of firing the machine gun.)

Chicago police sent dozens of men to check out every casino and liquor joint in Cicero. Cops took axes to gambling tables and roulette wheels and smashed blackboards used to record horse-racing results. They collected cases of beer and champagne and barrels of liquor. Dozens of men were arrested. They searched the house of Ralph Capone, Al's brother, and found an impressive stockpile of weapons, including machine-gun accessories, ammunition, and a variety of weapons. Four rifles were used as curtain rods in the front room. Shotguns were in the pantry, and three automatic pistols wrapped in silk were in the icebox. The police found a pearl-handled .25-caliber automatic pistol under the pillow of Ralph's wife and a .45 automatic under his.

Somewhere along the way—where isn't clear—police picked up a machine gun.

Al himself, however, had slipped out of town and was nowhere to be found.

At the Auto-Ordnance office in New York, John and Marcellus Thompson were shocked to hear that the Thompson gun was used in the murder of a public official. John paced his office with concern, while Marcellus hurried to board a train to Chicago.

"We designed that gun for law enforcement and military usage," Marcellus Thompson told Chicago reporters while he was in town. "I feel very sorry now to learn that one of them is in the hands of the lawless element. Its killing power is terrible."

The younger Thompson said he went straight to the police, where he examined the gun that police had picked up. Checking a secret serial number embedded in the gun, he traced it to Korecek's sporting-goods store.

The McSwiggin murder shocked many who thought Tommy guns were only a gangster problem. Hundreds turned out for his funeral on May 1, 1926.

Thompson headed to the shop himself, in a seedy side of town. The shop owner told Thompson he had sold a gun but didn't know the buyer.

Thompson shared the information with the police, who hauled Korecek in for questioning. For three days, they pestered him and trotted him out to face demanding reporters, trying to get him to cough up the names of the buyers. Korecek admitted that he had sold three guns, not one, but he begged the police to let him keep the buyers' names private.

"If I tell you, I'll die," he told them, weeping and shaking. "I sold these fellows one gun and then they said they'd kill me if I didn't get the others. Then, when they got them, they swore they'd take me for a ride if I ever squawked about them."

Korecek even pleaded to stay in jail rather than possibly face his customers. Ultimately, the police got a name—Charlie Carr, manager of a Capone bawdy house—but nothing more. Korecek survived.

Capone spent three months hanging out at a Michigan lake with friends while the dust settled in Chicago. In late July, he came back for a court hearing. There he denied any involvement in the shooting, and investigators didn't have any firm evidence. Anyone with information had gone mute or become forgetful. In a justice system swimming in bribery and corruption, a prosecution was all but impossible.

After a night in jail, Capone was let go.

The case was never solved.

A half-dozen shootings around the time of the McSwiggin killing were attributed to what police and the press called machine guns, including a barrage on a beauty shop that left it with more bullet holes

"than a man could have fired with a revolver in an hour." More were to come.

On a pleasant September afternoon five months after the Mc-Swiggin murder, Al Capone was enjoying lunch at a Cicero restaurant next to a local inn. A stream of cars approached. Like a marching band in a parade, the now-familiar growl and pop of guns started down the street and grew louder. Everyone in the restaurant dove to the floor.

Several cars slowly passed by, guns poking out from every window, spraying fire. When the last car arrived, a man in overalls stepped out with a Thompson gun, knelt down, and, like a conductor, finished the performance with a flourish by depositing a full magazine of bullets across the front of the building.

Police estimated that a thousand bullets had been fired. Luckily, only two bystanders were injured, though glass covered the ground. "It's a wonder no one was killed," Capone told reporters.

Less than a month later, the notorious gangster Hymie Weiss and an associate were gunned down in a storm of bullets on a street at midday near the Holy Name Cathedral. Two other associates were injured, as was a well-known criminal lawyer. The barrage of bullets was so intense that a Bible quotation inscribed on the cornerstone of the church was partly chipped away.

One of the gunners ditched a still-hot Thompson gun in the alley.

With that October shooting, Chicago newspapers counted at least forty-six people who had been killed in bootlegging wars thus far in 1926. The press also began to give the gun a list of nicknames: Chatterbox, Chicago Piano, Chopper, Chicago Typewriter. But the most common was just a simple play on the name: the Tommy gun.

In an editorial shortly after, the *Chicago Daily News* lamented that

A smiling Al Capone, in the mid-1920s

71

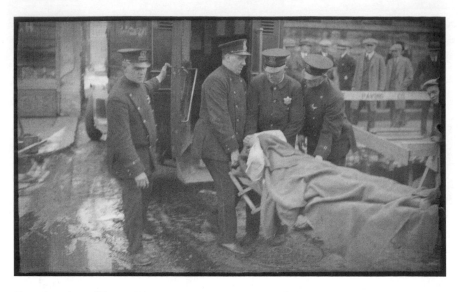

The shooting of Hymie Weiss and associates on a Chicago street finally prompted gangsters to discuss a ceasefire.

the easy money of Prohibition had not just introduced the machine gun, but also brought "to the streets of a great city the spectacle of four gangsters and a criminal lawyer shot down in the shadow of a cathedral . . ." That same easy money led police and city officials to take bribes and look away from crime and graft. The paper called on city leaders and citizens to step up to find the murderers and stop the corruption.

But with gangsters shooting gangsters, only one person really could make that move—Al Capone himself.

In an interview, Capone said he had nothing to do with Weiss's murder, but the "killing was unnecessary," he said. "I told Hymie time and again it was foolish for his North Side mob not to be friends with us in Cicero."

With Weiss gone, Capone said, "I'm ready to make peace any time."

Why? "I don't want to die in the street, punctured with machine-gun bullets," he told another reporter.

Chicago's bootleggers each claimed a piece of the city in the mid-1920s, and then fought violently to protect their territory.

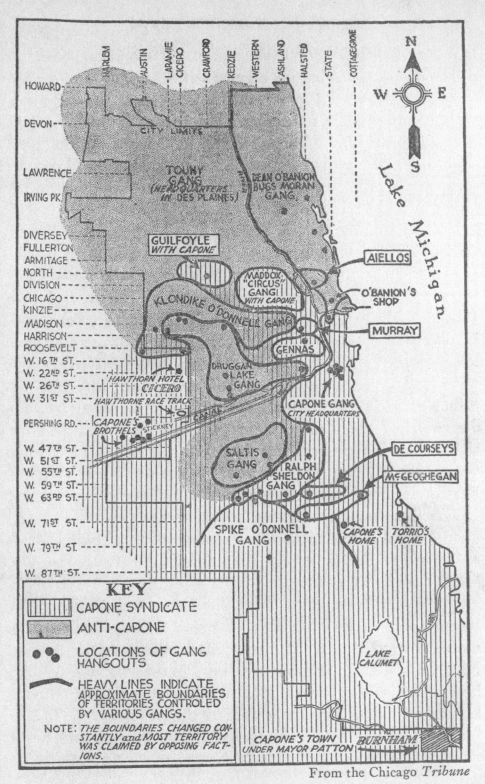

From the Chicago *Tribune*

ONE OF THE SEVERAL DIVISIONS OF
TERRITORY MADE BY THE GANGS

Shortly after, Capone helped to arrange a summit meeting of the remaining dealers in liquor and vice. There they agreed to a truce. They would each stick to their own territories.

"Gangland killings have come to an end in Chicago," Capone proclaimed. "Now, for the first time in two years, I will sleep without a gun under my pillow."

For about a year, the Tommy guns in Chicago were relatively silent. Unfortunately, that wasn't true everywhere.

CHAPTER 7

WILD TIGERS

FOR ALL THE KILLINGS, the increasing use of the Tommy gun in violent crimes in Chicago hadn't really pierced the national consciousness—at least along the East Coast.

But three days after Hymie Weiss was gunned down in October 1926, the brazen daylight attack on government employees and a U.S. mail truck in Elizabeth, New Jersey, felt like an attack on the country itself.

After John Enz was left dead on the pavement and two others were injured, President Coolidge was briefed on the shooting and robbery at a cabinet meeting. In a quick and forceful response, Coolidge dispatched more than 1,800 marines to all parts of the country to protect mail trucks, railcars, and rail terminals that moved mail. Citizens were warned to not loiter. The marines had orders "to shoot to kill when necessary."

Then, to fight fire with fire, Postmaster General Harry S. New ordered 250 new Thompson submachine guns to arm the marines.

While the federal government responded, state and local police in New Jersey fanned out to cover fourteen key roadways, stopping suspicious cars, particularly in the Watchung Mountains. Local farmers brought out their shotguns, muskets, and dusty weapons that hadn't been used in years to help form an impromptu posse. But no suspects were found.

Part of the case came to a bizarre end a few weeks later. In late October, police were called to an apartment in Detroit, Michigan, after neighbors heard gunshots.

The man who opened the door, William Crowley, murdered one policeman and wounded two others before being shot and killed himself. Inside, near empty champagne bottles, a stack of ten- and hundred-dollar bills totaling nearly $10,000 sat on a table.

In the bedroom, police found James Cunniffe, the leading suspect in the Elizabeth robbery, dead from several bullets. Next to him, a red-haired woman in a lavender dress was also dead; she had tried unsuccessfully to shield herself with her pocketbook, which contained more than $1,000—and a bullet hole.

A fight over how to divide the mail-robbery money had left all of them dead.

The horror and outrage over the Elizabeth murder sparked a pressing question: How did a Thompson submachine gun get into the killer's hands in the first place?

The simple answer: There were no regulations on the sale of Tommy guns, or any other machine gun. In fact, a gun expert told the *Newark*

Onlookers crowd around Tommy gun bullet holes left after the Elizabeth robbery.

"'AT'S THE BABY"

An October 1926 cartoon highlighted the new notoriety of the Thompson submachine gun.

Star-Eagle, the federal government had sold surplus guns at an auction, with no questions asked.

The rapid adoption of the automobile had led to new laws, and the invention and growth of radio had come with new regulations as well. But it hadn't occurred to anyone that civilians might use a recently invented military weapon on an American street.

Back in 1911, following an attempted assassination of New York City's mayor and the murder of a well-known novelist on a city sidewalk, the state of New York had adopted an unusually strict gun law. The Sullivan Act not only regulated carrying concealed weapons but also limited small-gun sales and ownership. The law required those buying revolvers or other concealable weapons to have a permit first, and it banned ownership by immigrants and those younger than sixteen. It also required a license from the police to carry a concealed weapon. Carrying an unlicensed concealed weapon became a felony.

Over the next several years, many other cities and states adopted similar laws, intended to restrict the small, out-of-sight weapons that were used more and more in crimes and suicides. The city of Chicago, too, required a special permit from police to buy a revolver or other small weapon.

Some people got around the laws by buying cheap handguns from mail-order catalogs in other states, until public concern pressured some magazines to drop the advertisements. The giant catalog retailer Sears, Roebuck and Co. stopped selling small guns in 1924. In 1927, Congress passed a law banning the sale of revolvers and other small guns through the mail, one of the country's first national gun laws. But it didn't have much impact, since buyers could use private delivery services or simply drive to another city themselves.

Unlike a pistol or revolver, the bigger, heavier Tommy gun was considered more like a rifle or shotgun, and those weren't covered under the concealed-weapons laws. So while the submachine gun was among the most powerful weapons in the world, and Auto-Ordnance might claim to be "on the side of law and order," the sporting-goods and hardware stores that sold it didn't have to worry about permits.

After the Elizabeth shooting, Owen P. White, a writer for *Collier's* weekly magazine, was aghast that even an honorable citizen could buy such "a diabolical engine of death," a weapon that could "stand off a whole platoon of policeman." He decided to see if he could buy a gun himself.

He visited several New York stores and each told him it would be happy to sell to him. He placed an order at one. But instead of receiving a gun, he got a visit from a detective. After a chat, the detective told him he could still buy the gun if he wanted, since there was no law preventing it.

In the case of the Elizabeth robbery, Marcellus Thompson told another *Collier's* reporter that a long-established New York sporting-goods house, "without a blemish on its reputation," had sold the gun.

The reporter pressed him. "Isn't there some way of keeping these machine guns out of the hands of criminals?"

Thompson was empathetic. "I know just how you feel when you ask that question," he answered. But, he said, "I don't know any way of stopping it. What can I do?"

Police need better arms, he said, and soldiers especially need better weapons. "We must have progress in arms for military purposes and for public safety just as we have progress in every other mechanical line," he explained. "In the next war, soldiers will be equipped, not with old-fashioned rifles, but with this machine gun or with one even more deadly."

Thompson explained that Auto-Ordnance needed to use distributors and retailers to sell the guns because they were the ones that could reach police departments, banks that needed to protect their funds, and companies that needed to protect payroll trucks. The company didn't try to monitor those sellers.

Even when Auto-Ordnance sold guns to factories, banks, and even law enforcement officers, the weapons didn't always stay there. Marcellus Thompson cited a former military man who owned a Midwestern mine. He had purchased three Thompsons that were kept locked in a safe. One night, twenty-five men barged into the office, broke open the safe, and stole the guns.

So, the reporter responded, each of those guns was hidden away and could be used at any time? Weren't they "like a wild tiger, ready to jump out and kill at a moment's notice"?

"That makes three more wild tigers loose somewhere," Thompson agreed.

By 1925, Auto-Ordnance had sold an estimated 3,000 of the 15,000 guns it had made, including some to foreign countries such as Belgium and Mexico. Of those, Marcellus Thompson and one of his dealers guessed that perhaps twelve to fifty had made their way into criminal hands in Chicago, likely a low estimate. In addition to Chicago, one showed up in a gang shoot-out in Long Beach, California, and another in a rum-running exchange in the waters off Long Island, New York. Tommy guns had also been used—or soon would be—in crimes in Philadelphia, Detroit, St. Louis, and New York City, where a longtime gangster was mowed down on a city street.

Some dealers still insisted they didn't sell to just anyone. One Chicago dealer told a reporter that he wouldn't sell to a thug, but added, "you're a magazine writer. I know you're not going to kill anybody with it." The same dealer, however, also bragged about discriminating based on race. One day, a preacher called him about buying a Thompson gun. When the caller turned out to be a black man, the dealer notified the police, who told him to sell the weapon and they would take it from there.

After the man bought the gun and left the store, police arrested him and confiscated his gun. "There wasn't anything they could do with him, so he was examined for his sanity for about a week and turned loose," the dealer said proudly.

Gangsters had it much easier. If they were turned away, they simply went to a neighboring state. Or a middleman bought the guns and then resold them to gangsters at a higher price.

At the same time, police forces that bought the guns were increasingly reluctant to use them because their rapid fire raised the chances of hurting innocent people. "We can't turn loose an endless stream of bullets down a crowded thoroughfare," one police official said.

Inside Auto-Ordnance, John Thompson added a handwritten note for a colleague on a magazine article about the Elizabeth robbery, indicating his desire that dealers restrict sales to law enforcement:

> *As you have asserted, there is no desire on the part of the A.O. Corp. for civilian use of the T.S.M.G. Its use should be confined by law to Governments—National, State, County and Municipal. Yours on the side of law and order.*
>
> *Everywhere. J.T.T. 11-24-26*

But that was largely wishful thinking. Auto-Ordnance might urge its dealers to sell only to those "on the side of law and order," but neither John nor Marcellus Thompson ever put any restrictions on dealers or their sales. For a short time, some East Coast dealers may have paid more attention to their buyers. But without any official restrictions, the pause wouldn't last.

CHAPTER 8
VALENTINES AND VIOLINS

THE **TOMMY GUNS IN CHICAGO** could stay quiet only so long, in part because they were so easy to buy.

Peter von Frantzius was a long-established sporting-goods dealer in Chicago when a man who called himself Frank Thompson walked into his shop. Von Frantzius, a small man with a thin mustache and a law degree from Northwestern University, sold a wide range of guns in his store, from revolvers to German machine guns to the Thompson sub-machine gun.

Initially, von Frantzius told authorities that he believed Frank Thompson owned his own sporting-goods store in Kirkland, Illinois, and had his own legitimate customers. A few days later, von Frantzius changed his story. Business had been bad, he admitted, and he needed sales. He had arranged to sell the guns to Thompson at a wholesale price, taking a profit of only $55 a gun instead of a more typical profit of up to $90 a gun. He gave Thompson the guns in Chicago. But then, to make the sales look more legitimate, he shipped bricks to towns in northern Illinois so that it would appear the guns had been sent there.

Thompson's parents told police that their son was selling cemetery plots and life insurance policies. In truth, the thirty-eight-year-old was a middleman who bought guns from dealers and resold them to gangsters willing to pay top dollar for powerful weapons. Thompson picked up two Tommy guns from von Frantzius in October 1928, two more on January 28, 1929, and the final two on February 2.

Then, on the cold morning of February 14, 1929, four men walked into a Chicago warehouse, two in police uniforms and two in plain clothes. Inside the chilly building were several members of Bugs Moran's gang, another of Chicago's successful bootleggers. Moran was expected but hadn't yet made it over.

When the four walked in, the Moran men figured they were part of a routine Prohibition bust. The police would harass them and maybe arrest them, but they would be back together within hours. So they lined up facing one wall and put their hands in the air.

Within seconds, two of the men opened fire with Thompson guns. One would drive fifty bullets into the defenseless men and the wall behind them, while the other delivered twenty shots in a single roar. With their bodies riddled with ammunition, most of the men fell right where they were. Six died right away. A seventh died later that day.

When the howl of the guns quieted, the four shooters walked out quickly, with the men in uniforms pointing their now-emptied guns at the backs of the other two so it would look as if police were escorting crooks out of the garage. They drove away in a Cadillac that resembled a police detective car, leaving behind a smoky room, rivers of blood, and a wailing dog still tied to a truck.

The gory aftermath of the St. Valentine's Day Massacre shocked even jaded Chicago policemen.

Even experienced Chicago police were unprepared for the grisly scene of what became known as the St. Valentine's Day Massacre. Chicago residents, long used to gangsters murdering gangsters, couldn't imagine who would mow down seven men at once while their backs were turned. Despite all the previous gangster violence in Chicago, the nation was horrified that the graft and greed of Prohibition had led to this kind of slaughter.

Suspicions, of course, turned to Al Capone, but he was living comfortably in Miami, Florida, thousands of miles from the crime. Gangsters were picked up, including those with ties to Capone, and questioned. But without hard evidence, they were let go.

In the weeks after the vicious shooting, John Stege, now deputy commissioner of the Chicago police, brought in three men, including von Frantzius, who he said had sold a total of one hundred submachine guns to gangsters. Peter von Frantzius was quizzed into the night—and then questioned again. At first he admitted selling a total of eleven Thompson guns, including two guns to a man with a fake Indiana police badge, and a gun to a suburban police officer, who delivered it to a Capone-owned dog-racing track. Then, von Frantzius confessed to selling a total of twenty submachine guns. As an extra service, he would grind the serial number off a gun.

Charges were never filed against him. Nothing he had done was actually illegal.

Another seller had ordered his guns directly from New York, saying he was buying them for a Mexican rebel army, when they were actually going to gangsters.

But, Stege complained, he couldn't keep the men because "there was no law violated," even though "those guns will be used against policemen and in bank robberies."

In one inquiry, von Frantzius was asked whether he cared where the guns went.

"No," he answered. "We are in the business of selling firearms."

To help crack the massacre case, the police turned to Calvin H. Goddard, a medical doctor who had become an expert on matching bullets and cartridge cases with the guns that fired them. Goddard had adapted medical tools designed for looking inside a person's lungs and other hard-to-see body parts so that he could study the inside of a gun barrel.

Trying to find the shooters responsible for 1929 massacre, Coroner Herman Bundesen (with glasses) and colleagues shot bullets into cotton and then studied them for markings unique to each Tommy gun.

There he learned that each gun made a unique mark on the ammunition, allowing him to connect a fired bullet to a particular weapon.

As police identified guns sold by von Frantzius and others, the guns' buyers offered to bring them in for testing. Nothing matched.

When an Auto-Ordnance official offered to help police trace those guns, Stege had sharp words for him: "I told him the only help he could give was to go back and close the gun factory," Stege said. "The weapons are absolutely of no value to police, banks, guards, messengers, or anyone other than criminals."

The Illinois legislature had previously considered—and rejected—banning machine guns, concerned that they "may be sold with as much freedom as water pistols."

This time, with the gory crime still fresh, legislators approved a law in June 1929 forbidding the purchase, possession, or transportation of machine guns. They made an exception for the military and were ready to make one for the police. But Stege believed so strongly that innocent people would be injured if police used the weapons that he persuaded lawmakers to ban them even for law enforcement.

The Illinois governor believed law enforcement officers should be able to own the guns, so he vetoed the bill. The Thompson remained a legal weapon.

A break in the massacre case came unexpectedly in December 1929, when two drivers collided in a small traffic accident in western Michigan. When a police officer tried to help, one driver pulled out a gun and killed him before driving off.

The car was later abandoned, and papers found in it led police to the home of Fred "Killer" Burke, a longtime bank robber and violent thug. There police found money from a recent Wisconsin bank robbery and an impressive arsenal, including revolvers, piles of ammunition, and two Tommy guns.

The weapons were sent to Chicago for testing. Just before Christmas, Goddard delivered some surprising news: These Tommy guns recovered in Michigan were the two used in the horrific Valentine's Day crime. Further, one of the guns had been used to blow away a famous gangster on a New York street in 1928.

Oddly, though, Fred Burke was never charged—or even questioned—in any of those crimes. When police finally caught up with him in 1931, he was convicted for murdering the police officer and spent the rest of his life in a Michigan prison.

In 1931, law enforcement, with help from the federal government,

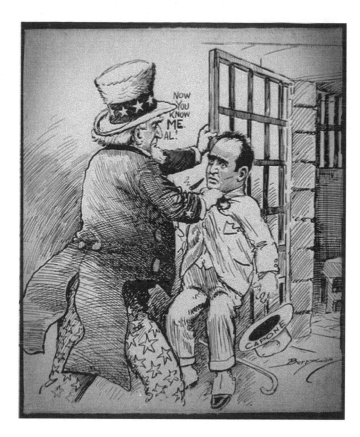

Uncle Sam introduces himself to Al Capone in a 1931 Clifford K. Berryman cartoon.

would, however, finally catch up with Al Capone—though not for violent crimes. He was convicted of failing to pay income taxes on his vast gambling and bootlegging empire and sentenced to eleven years in prison.

Despite numerous rumors, theories, conspiracies, and even some indictments, no one was ever convicted or even formally connected to the St. Valentine's Day murders. In fact, there was only a single certain participant in one of the most notorious crimes of the twentieth century: the Thompson submachine gun. Now, around the nation and around the world, virtually everyone knew what an effective killer it was.

The year 1929 turned out to be an eventful one in many ways. Americans were tiring of Prohibition, and the bloody St. Valentine's Day shooting sped up the shift in public opinion against the Eighteenth Amendment.

Despite Prohibition, the stock market had been roaring throughout the 1920s, bringing prosperity to those who played it. But in September 1929, it began to slide. In October it crashed, wiping out billions of dollars in wealth in a short time. Business had already been slowing, but now it began to brake to a near halt. Thousands of people lost their jobs as both wealthy individuals and companies cut back to make ends meet. The United States headed into the Great Depression.

In late 1928, Thomas Fortune Ryan died at the age of seventy-seven, after funding the company and the Thompsons for a dozen years. By then, more than 6,000 submachine guns had been sold, leaving more than 8,000 still gathering dust in a warehouse. Marcellus Thompson continued to look for legitimate new buyers and tried to win more support from the U.S. military.

Ryan's heirs and the lawyer overseeing his estate, a pacifist named Elihu Root, weren't much interested in "the sale of man-killers" or the attention they seemed to get. Walter B. Ryan, Jr., a nephew of Ryan's, was put in charge of Auto-Ordnance, and both John and Marcellus Thompson were effectively pushed out. In late 1930, the company shut down its sales force. It insisted from then on that it would sell only to military and law enforcement buyers. While guns already in circulation could be sold again and again, new sales slowed to a trickle.

But even as the company seemed to wind down, the fame and reputation of its prominent weapon grew. The shocking 1929 murders had piqued the fascination of a nation—and caught the attention of Hollywood. Movies had just begun to add sound, perfect for highlighting the squeal of tires on a getaway car and the distinctive rat-a-tat-tat of a machine gun.

In the early 1930s, Hollywood began to crank out gangster movies, producing an estimated fifty such movies in 1931. These movies created unlikely stars such as James Cagney and Edward G. Robinson—squat, tough-looking men who oozed charisma and swagger on the big screen. Usually the Tommy gun, with its distinctive round magazine, got a starring role, too.

Edward G. Robinson, in his breakthrough role in *Little Caesar,* barely escapes Tommy gun fire.

Religious and some civic leaders fretted that showing the crooks with money, fame, and beautiful girlfriends glorified the bad guys, even though the main character usually died violently at the end, a not-so-subtle moral reminder about the cost of crime. But at a time when more than half of America—an estimated ninety million people a week—went to the movies, audiences gobbled them up.

In one of the first blockbuster gangster films, *Little Caesar,* Edward G. Robinson played Caesar Enrico Bandello, a ruthless killer modeled on Al Capone. The film made Robinson a star, which he attributed later to "the public preoccupation with the American dream of success. Rico was a guy who came from poverty and made it big . . . [E]veryone could identify with his climb."

Making such movies at a time before fancy cameras and special effects was challenging. Robinson was uncomfortable with guns and blinked every time he fired one. Finally, the director put tape on his eyelids to keep them open during crucial scenes. The machine gun shot blank bullets—but they were still projectiles, and steel plates were pinned inside Robinson's clothing to protect him. Even so, he had trouble staying still and narrowly avoided injury.

In capturing the stories, Hollywood plucked a detail from the news and turned it into a well-known myth about the Tommy gun. As far back as 1916, a robber had concealed a sawed-off shotgun in a violin case. In 1927, a former Atlanta policeman used a sawed-off shotgun hidden in a violin case to shoot a prominent investigator in a hotel. Sawed-off shotguns are shortened to be more easily concealed, and a few times over the next few years in Newark and Chicago, crooks pulled them from violin cases before opening fire.

In March 1929, according to some news accounts, two neatly dressed young men opened violin cases on a Chicago-area train and pulled out machine guns. While one man kept passengers at bay, the other hit a bank official with the gun and snatched his satchel, which was stuffed with checks. The robbers and two accomplices then escaped to a waiting car.

Chicago police Captain John Stege holds a violin case with a dismantled Tommy gun—which doesn't quite fit in the space.

Whether the report is true isn't clear. Another account says the men used trombone cases, and a third account described the weapons as sawed-off shotguns. As a *Chicago Daily News* photo from the late 1920s shows, a Tommy gun doesn't fit in a violin case unless it is dismantled, and even then, the case may not close.

Regardless, the idea captured a filmmaker's imagination. An early gangster movie from 1930, *The Doorway to Hell*, featured James Cagney in his second film role and made reference (offscreen) to the St. Valentine's Day murders. The movie opens with a hit man retrieving his violin case from behind a pool-hall counter. "I'm going out to teach a guy a lesson," he says. Soon after, he opens the violin case in a car and assembles a machine gun to take care of an enemy.

Censors in New York and Ohio actually cut out the scene of the gun in the case, fearful it would teach crooks something new. But it didn't take long for many people to simply assume that Thompson guns were carried in violin cases. Later, some gangsters may actually have copied the idea from the movies.

Real musicians were frequently teased about what they were actually carrying, and Tommy-hiding violin cases became the punch line in cartoons and jokes. But as the nation's economic troubles deepened, the gun's raw power was increasingly felt beyond the gangster world—and that was no laughing matter.

CHAPTER 9

ATTACK AND INTIMIDATION

WHILE CHICAGO OFFICIALS seemed to look the other way, officials in New York, home to the Sullivan law, quickly lost patience with the Thompson gun once New York City's gangsters adopted it in the early 1930s.

On a steaming hot evening in July 1931, a street in Little Italy was filled with children playing. Frank Scalesi, a fourteen-year-old with red hair, was selling lemonade for a penny a glass outside a private social club. A man was lounging near the club door.

In the early evening, a touring car slowed down in front of the club and gun barrels suddenly poked out. A "sharp crackling like the explosions of a string of fire crackers" sent the children screaming and running. The man in front of the club hit the ground, escaping injury. Frank Scalesi's lemonade pitcher shattered.

When the car passed, five-year-old Michael Vengalli had been fatally injured. His seven-year-old brother was hit five times by shotgun

New York Governor Franklin D. Roosevelt addresses a special legislative session in August 1931.

pellets. Three other children were wounded, including a three-year-old who had been asleep in a carriage.

Though no one wanted to assist police in identifying the shooters, parents denounced the gangsters and "their terrorism." In Albany, New York, Governor Franklin D. Roosevelt called the shooting a "damnable" outrage. Newspapers dubbed it the "Baby Massacre" and sensationally followed every clue about the gangland shooting.

Witnesses reported the rapid fire of a machine gun, though police weren't convinced one had been used. It didn't really matter. The Tommy gun was now considered the culprit in every especially violent shooting.

When New York legislators met during a special session in September, New York's acting mayor and its police commissioner asked for stiffer laws for both machine guns and pistols, which remained a significant crime problem. They sought to fingerprint pistol owners and outlaw the sale or possession of machine guns, except to the military or law enforcement.

"There is no good reason why anyone outside the militia or the peace officers of the state should need a machine gun," Police Commissioner Edward Mulrooney told legislators.

Governor Roosevelt put his full support behind the bills. He even shared a personal story: He once narrowly avoided a tragedy when he almost fired a shotgun at an employee, thinking he was a burglar. Merely owning a gun could lead to that kind of danger, he told reporters.

The gun laws passed the New York legislature within a few weeks— though Tommy guns didn't completely disappear from the streets.

In October, twenty-three-year-old Vincent Coll, an ambitious and dangerous beer baron, was brought to trial for the "Baby Massacre." But the key witness turned out to be unreliable and Coll was acquitted.

Vincent Coll, who was tried for the "Baby Massacre"

Other gangsters chose their own form of justice to eliminate their competition. In February 1932, Coll entered a drugstore with a bodyguard to use a pay telephone in the back. Soon after, a man walked into the store with a Tommy gun, telling the clerks and customers to stay calm. He headed toward the phone booth while Coll's bodyguard slipped out of the store.

"Turn around, Vincent," the gunner said, "and get ready for it."

When Coll turned, the man pulled the trigger, filling him with lead.

Coll crumpled onto the floor of the small booth. The gunner quickly left the store. Even after all the outrageous violence of the Prohibition years, the cold-blooded murder in a phone booth made for yet another round of sensational headlines.

A newspaper map offers details of the murder of gangster Vincent Coll in a drugstore phone booth.

In 1933, in the depths of the Great Depression, political winds were shifting. By the end of the year, Prohibition would be over. But the nation's economic woes created another controversial market for the Thompson submachine gun: companies facing labor trouble.

In the 1920s, before workers had the legally protected right to organize, companies often called on states to send out the National Guard when their workers banded together to protest, call strikes, or otherwise challenge their low pay or dangerous working conditions—especially if the workers hinted at violence. Those military units frequently brought along impressive military weapons, such as World War I–era machine guns, and sometimes fired on workers.

Compared with bigger military weapons, the Tommy gun was easy to buy, so companies or their local sheriffs could pick up one or two from Auto-Ordnance or a dealer for their own use. As early as 1921, companies in the steel, textile, coal, and other mining industries bought Thompson guns, primarily when workers were threatening strikes or just starting one. In 1922, during five months of coal strikes across twenty-one states, a coal company in Birmingham, Alabama, bought four guns; Sunlight Mining Company of Chicago bought two; and a Tennessee coal company picked up five.

Similarly, during a series of coal strikes in 1927 and 1928, at least five companies bought Tommy guns, presumably to protect their property. Pittsburgh Coal Company, owned by R. B. Mellon and his brother, Treasury Secretary Andrew Mellon, broke with its mine workers' union in 1925, hiring new workers at lower pay and forming its own armed police force. The company already owned three Thompson submachine guns, but it also purchased tear gas, revolvers, and other arms for its new force.

In a Senate hearing investigating the coal industry in 1928, a questioner asked R. B. Mellon if he would approve of his police having machine guns.

"The same as police here have?" Mellon responded.

"Well, would you approve of that?" he was asked.

"It is necessary," he answered. "You could not run without them."

Quickly, then, he backed away from his comment, saying, "I don't know anything about machine guns."

After investigating years of submachine gun sales to mining and other industrial companies, another U.S. Senate committee would note in the late 1930s that the Thompson gun wasn't much of a defensive firearm. Rather, the committee said, it "is the gangster's weapon, intended not for defense but for sudden attack and wholesale intimidation or slaughter."

In 1932, after new Thompson orders had slipped to next to nothing, the Ryan family turned over sales to Federal Laboratories, Inc., of Pittsburgh, Pennsylvania, which also sold tear gas, canister-firing rifles, and other riot gear to police and companies with labor issues. Trying to avoid more embarrassing publicity about the Tommy gun, the Ryan family and Auto-Ordnance required Federal Laboratories to sell only to law enforcement or to companies that weren't involved in strikes. It even insisted buyers sign sworn statements that they wouldn't transfer the gun to someone else after they bought it. But the sales company either ignored the policy or found ways around it.

Federal Laboratories sold the guns aggressively to countries facing revolution or war, such as Cuba, Bolivia, and Paraguay, and also marketed the guns, along with its other products, to mining firms, mills, steel companies, and others facing labor unrest. Amid the Depression, workers increasingly protested lowered wages, reduced hours,

John W. Young (right), president of Federal Laboratories, with his secretary, G. Oberdick

or efforts to replace current workers with those so desperate that they would take less pay.

Federal Laboratories urged its salesmen to watch news reports of labor conflicts and to be willing to work through the night or early in the morning to sell its products to worried companies.

When a Senate committee later grilled him about that policy, John W. Young, the company's president, answered, "That is a part of our sales work, to get business where there is a demand for our product."

After Franklin D. Roosevelt became president in 1933, he introduced New Deal laws intended to protect workers' rights to form unions and to bring both company officials and workers to the bargaining table. Efforts to organize expanded and strikes increased. But many company executives, feeling threatened by unions, simply refused to acknowledge workers' new rights. Some hired spies and strikebreakers to report on and harass their employees or rough up organizers and their supporters.

In October 1933, Rex Coal Company, grappling with a strike in Illinois, approached Federal Laboratories about buying a Thompson gun.

A sales executive explained that it couldn't sell to Rex under Auto-Ordnance rules. "There is only one 'out,' " he wrote, "and that is for the sheriff to order the gun on his official order forms, and have the county sign to the effect that the gun will not be transferred without the permission of the manufacturer."

But then, he continued, if the county wanted "to loan the gun to you, that, of course, would be a deal between you and the County, and we would have no chance to counsel with you on it."

That apparently was enough. The sheriff bought the gun—paid for by Rex Coal.

Around the same time, Young was called to Ambridge, Pennsylvania, the site of ongoing labor disputes between workers and three steel mills. There, Young said, county commissioners complained about workers with clubs and bricks and told him in a meeting that they "wanted 200 shotguns to clear up the situation, if need be, even if they had to kill 15 or 20 people."

Young said he protested, telling the commissioners, "in this day and age, that should not be tried," and urged them to encourage workers to put down their sticks and rocks.

Despite his stance, Young then sold tear gas to area steel companies and four Thompson guns to the sheriff's office. One of the steel companies paid for the guns and 3,000 rounds of ammunition.

Shortly after the sale, more than 200 citizens deputized as sheriffs and armed with riot sticks, tear gas, and at least one Tommy gun

A front-page photograph shows a deputy armed with a Tommy gun trying to disarm a picketing worker.

Pittsburgh Sun-Telegraph

NIGHT WALL ST CLOSING PRICES

Only Pittsburgh Newspaper Printing International News Service Dispatches

ESTAB. 1927 — VOL. 13—NO. 66   48 PAGES   FRIDAY, OCTOBER 6, 1933   THREE CENTS

ROOSEVELT CALLS STEEL LEADERS IN MOVE TO HALT MINE WARFARE

GIANTS LEAD NATS IN FOURTH BATTLE OF WORLD SERIES

SCORE BY INNINGS

	R.	H.	E.
N. Y.	000 100	—	
Wash.	000 000	—	

Batteries—Hubbell and Mancuso, Weaver and Sewell.

By CHARLES J. DOYLE
Staff Correspondent

GRIFFITH STADIUM, WASHINGTON, Oct. 6.—The New York Giants, champions of the National League, were leading the Washington Senators, champions of the American League, in the fourth battle of the 1933 World Series here this afternoon.

Carl Hubbell, star southpaw of the Giants, who defeated the Senators in the first game at New York, made his second start of the series, while Monte Weaver was selected by Manager Joe Cronin of the Nats.

The same was almost five minutes late in starting. Monte Weaver making his first World Series start, had trouble locating *(Continued on Page Forty-one, Col. 4.)*

Play-by-Play Detail Of Fourth Series Game

GRIFFITH STADIUM, WASHINGTON, Oct. 6.—(AP)—The play-by-play account of the fourth battle of the World Series between the New York Giants and Washington Senators here this afternoon follows:

FIRST INNING

GIANTS—Moore up Ball 1 high and outside Ball 2 outside Ball 3 high. Cronin came in for a short talk with Weaver. Strike 1 called Moore walked, the fourth ball being inside Crits up—Strike 1 called Ball 1 it was a pitch out Critz lined into a double play. Myer to Kuhel Myer caught the drive and fired to Kuhel before the runner could return to the base. Terry up—Strike 1 called Ball 1 outside drive 2 called. It was a foul ball that cut the inside corner of the plate Terry *(Continued on Page Forty-one, Col. 3.)*

WALL STREET PROBE NAMES J. H. HILLMAN

WASHINGTON, Oct. 6.—(AP)—Senator Couzens (Rep.) of Michigan, charged before Senate investigators today that some "wise guys unloaded" more than $41,000,000 of railroad stock during the boom in 1929 on an investment trust organized by Dillon, Read & Co.

That assertion by the member of the stock market inquiry committee followed disclosure that investments by the trusts in two railroads, both of which later went into receivership, had depreciated to almost nothing.

Named in the proceedings was J. H. Hillman, Jr. of Pittsburgh. The stock was acquired by joint accounts between the trusts and accounts of the trusts in 1929 managed by the latter.

"Same wise guys must have been unloading on you, there is no doubt of that," said Couzens. *(Continued on Page Eighteen, Col. 2.)*

STOCK EXCHANGES FACE U. S. CONTROL

NEW YORK, Oct. 6.—(AP)—A committee to consider drafting legislation to put securities exchanges under federal control has been appointed by Commerce Secretary Roper, it was learned in Wall Street today.

"This was confirmed by A. A. Berle, Jr., a member of the committee, who said at his office that the group had been appointed at the request of President Roosevelt 'to consider the advisability of formulating legislation for submission to Congress looking toward supervision of the New York Stock Exchange and other security exchanges by the federal government.'"

In addition to Berle, who is been a prominent member of the "brains trust," it was understood the members of the committee will be Arthur H. Dean, member of the New York law firm of Sullivan and Cromwell; John Dickinson, Assistant Secretary of Commerce; Dean Acheson, Under Secretary of the Treasury; Arthur J. Richardson, Washington lawyer.

EX-SECRETARY SUES IRA BASSETT ESTATE

Notice of suit against Genieve M. Mark, administrator of the estate of Ira S. Bassett, millionaire man enamelist, was filed in the prothonotary's office by Attorney Jacob S. Hill in behalf of Gertrude Woodward, of Perrysville.

Mrs. Woodward, former confidential secretary to Bassett, understood to claim the sum of money is due her from the estate. Bassett, after a turbulent career, died two years ago, reputedly wealthy. Creditors were unable to find trace of his supposed wealth.

Police Ban Halloween Pranks

Police Supt. Franklin T. McQuade put his foot down today on all malicious pre-Halloween pranks.

He sent out a general order to arrest all persons caught carrying off porch furniture, gates, soaping automobile windows or the like. Those destroying property will be arrested on a charge of malicious mischief.

McQuade said:

"We have no objections to boys having fun during this season, but we will not permit or tolerate them to destroy property or annoy or molest people. If the boys engage in clean fun we will not annoy them. But just as soon as they become rowdies then the police will take action."

'Cycle Crash Hurts Austrian Prince

VIENNA, Oct. 6.—(AP)—Prince Rudolf of Windischgraetz, great-grandson of the late Empress Franz Josef, was injured critically in a motorcycle accident here today.

The Prince is an employe of an automobile company.

Deputies, Machine Gun-Equipped, Disarming an Ambridge 'Picket'

—Turn to Page Three for Full-Page Picture Story of the Ambridge Warring—

Deputies, one armed with a machine gun, in the tussle to disarm one Mr. Beniamo, alias Benny Beans, Aliquippa, arrested and charged with drawing this wicked automatic pistol on them when they found him crouched in bushes as 200 deputies under Sheriff Charles O'Laughlin cleared out the strike picket lines at Ambridge. He is also charged with attempting to stab Chief Deputy Joe Stone. This is a Sun-Telegraph picture.

GRIM QUIET COVERS AMBRIDGE RIOT ZONE

A grim, forced quiet settled over Ambridge today in the wake of death and panic.

Outside the Spang - Chalfant plant 50 deputy sheriffs, guns in hand, patrolled yesterday's battlefield, on which not more than a dozen pickets were to be seen today.

They stood there, specters in the fog, as the dawn came up, but the townspeople the strike symbolism came knew the strength of those ready weapons.

They were from Beaver County, those deputies, and they marched to the mill district, scattering any crowds which gathered. Two hundred deputies had orders to keep the streets clear and they were carrying them out.

In groups of 10 they moved about the streets and alleys near the mill district, walking any crowds which gathered.

Communists they had been warned were trying to organize their union in the Ambridge plants.

They kept the cordons moving smartly in Duss avenue today. When one, a man of 50 refused with an oath to tell them his business, he was kicked and dragged. This was the only clash seen today.

(Continued on Page Three, Col. 8.)

MELLON BIOGRAPHER FREED IN RIOT CASE

After occupying a chilly police cell overnight, Harvey O'Connor, 36, who quarreled into the spotlight as the author of "Mellon's Millions," was freed today after being suspected of having some connection with yesterday's fatal rioting in Ambridge.

Dressed as a laborer in a soiled workshirt, gray sweater and old blue serge trousers, the author was arrested and dragged from custody by Judge W. Heber Dithrich in habeas corpus proceedings.

Harkins told the court he had arrested O'Connor late yesterday in his home, 314 Maryland avenue, Aliquippa, on a "John Doe" warrant charging inciting to riot lodged by an Ambridge justice of the peace. He said he had instructions to arrest the author of a riot inciting Communist license PF293, seen yesterday in *(Continued on Page Eighteen)*

JOHNSON IN PARLEY WITH PRESIDENT ON STRIKE

BULLETIN.

WASHINGTON, Oct. 6.—(AP)—President Roosevelt today called representatives of the steel industry to a White House conference tomorrow in an effort to solve the difficulties between operators and workers in the steel corporation's mines in Western Pennsylvania.

WASHINGTON, Oct. 6.—(AP)—After a two-hour conference on the Pennsylvania coal strikes, Hugh S. Johnson, NRA administrator, today went to the White House to discuss the situation with the Chief Executive.

Johnson left at his own office Gov. Pinchot of Pennsylvania, John L. Lewis, president of the United Mine Workers, and others, who continued their parleying. Leaving the NRA quarters, Johnson told newsmen he could make no comment on the situation.

Among the conferees in his office were Edward F. McGrady, assistant administrative and assistant Secretary of Labor, and Gerard Swope, Walter Teagle and George L. Berry, the latter president of the Pressmen's Union.

These three compose a coal arbitration board which had been set up last July to iron out differences in the five Pennsylvania coal strike pending adoption of a code.

Their functions had been considered ended since the code may be in force, sets up a system of coal labor boards, which are to begin operations by October 12.

Their presence in the conference, however, gave rise to the intimation that the administration is considering some immediate recovery step to end the miners, get the strikers back to work.

Gov. Pinchot told newsmen that the only way workers' hunger could would be to force them to the code—that would throw.

The suspension center workers in the "captive" mines of the steel corporations.

Although the workers are demanding recognition of their union before returning to their jobs, officials familiar with the code are almost sure to *(Continued on Page Two, Col. 1.)*

2 DEPUTIES, STRIKE SHOT AT FRICK PI

By AL GOUGH

UNIONTOWN, Pa., Oct. 6.—State police patrolled two bullet-scarred towns of the Frick-owned Colonial mines today after a night of terror.

Two major engagements in which pickets and semi-union workers exchanged gunfire for more than an hour resulted in the wounding of two company deputies and one striker. Four pickets were arrested, charged with carrying firearms.

More than 1,000 shots were exchanged. None of the wounded was serious. The deputies, Clifford Hall and J. W. Frederick, were treated on the scene, mained on duty. The unidentified, received scratch when a bullet hand. He refused then tention and disappeared.

The three Run Colonial mines died with bullets and pistols opened by the co pickets looked like a full of bullet holes.

Conflicting reports to police concerning the trouble. The occurred about 10 o'clock as the deputies that came from the houses. The wounded. *(Continued on Page Two)*

A. F. L. BLOCKS PRA FOR MINE STRIKE

WASHINGTON, Oct. 6.—(AP)—Half a dozen delegates today blocked introduction of a resolution at the American Federation of Labor convention indorsing efforts of coal mine strikers and censuring union officials who asked them in return to work without guarantees their their requests have been fulfilled.

Because of convention rules, the resolution presented by Reuben Burg, representing a cleaners, dyers, spotters and pressers union required unanimous consent. Half a dozen delegates were on their feet objecting when the resolution had been read.

Delegates and federation officials interpreted the convention's action to mean it indorsed the plans of President Willi for industrial peace and for recovery as applying to the program.

As proposed, the would have put the coal mine strikers' recovery is supporting heroic efforts to reawake standard of living and calling full of bullet holes.

It also would have say and all union mine call the mine workers work without that demands granted," and would all affiliated unions national unions to give support to the deadlock being waged by the mine

QUESTION HUSBAN OF BULLET VIC

Robert Soler, of Jenny Lind street, McKeesport, was brought to the District Attorney's office early today for questioning in connection with the mysterious death of his wife, Mrs. La Soler, last Sunday.

County Detectives who said Soler was brought after Harry B. Ullom, county detectives.

Mrs. Soler, mother of five found moaning in her bed heart shortly be found moaning in *(Continued on Page Eighteen)*

charged picketers in Ambridge. A man was killed, at least ten others were shot, and some were beaten up in the melee.

The next year, Federal Laboratories sold four submachine guns to the police of West Point, Georgia, which immediately turned them over to the West Point Manufacturing Company, violating the sales agreement. West Point, which ran cotton mills, didn't even have labor problems at the time. But it also borrowed three more Tommy guns from a coal company. It persuaded the sheriff to deputize about 800 men as special police and arm them all with some kind of weapon. Then it turned them loose among five communities where it had mills to intimidate workers and discourage them from ever flexing their union muscle.

Some of the thugs blocked the one road between the towns, at one point shooting out a doctor's tires with one of the Tommy guns. Some simply pointed Tommy guns at people and warned them to move on. One dry-cleaning businessman, Ester Lee Groover, picked up some suits from four guards at a boardinghouse and was accused of being a labor sympathizer. With machine guns nearby, one guard knocked him down repeatedly and another put a gun in his face, before telling him "we do not want to hear any more of this union agitating around here."

Altogether, at least 249 Thompson guns were sold to 122 companies or individuals with company ties between 1921 and 1934—but none to any labor unions. Sometimes, guns were sold for cash to avoid a paper trail or invoices were doctored to hide what companies were buying. Some companies built up stocks of tear gas and guns that were much greater than those of city police forces. But those details wouldn't be disclosed until the later 1930s, during a series of Senate hearings. Then, senators raised serious questions about why any company needed an arsenal, especially of military weapons, and why employers operated private police forces that went beyond protecting their own mills and mines.

At the time that these labor and industry battles were heating up in the early 1930s, however, most Americans were just worried about getting jobs or keeping them. Unemployment was sky-high and banks were failing. As economic troubles multiplied, distrust of authority grew. In those troubled times, Tommy guns would end up in a new set of hands and earn a different kind of attention.

CHAPTER 10
THE WAR ON CRIME

PROHIBITION HAD SPAWNED a generation of gun-toting gangsters intent on building—and protecting—illegal enterprises in liquor and beer. But the Depression created a different kind of violent gang: often poor and poorly educated men (and some women), who turned to stealing, car theft, and later armed bank robbery to get by.

The few dozen who got away with it made headlines as their crimes—and their Tommy guns—exploded into national prominence.

Newspapers and crime magazines, hungry for entertaining stories, tracked their every move, sometimes embellishing details or speculating on their next steps without any evidence. The gangs were hated and reviled in some circles while earning a level of admiration and fame in others. Bystanders who found themselves in banks as they were robbed or knew people who faced the barrel of a gun must have been terrified. But to many others, the Depression-era bandits were endlessly fascinating, almost like watching an action movie unfold.

In the early 1930s, Charles Arthur Floyd was something of a celebrity in his home state of Oklahoma. He had spent five years in prison for stealing a St. Louis, Missouri, store's payroll in 1925 and tried to go straight afterward. But when the police kept accusing him of crimes, he turned to robbing banks.

By 1932, at the age of twenty-eight, he was accused of holding up at least twenty banks in eastern Oklahoma, though he couldn't possibly have hit all the banks that the newspapers pinned on him. He was also credited with introducing the submachine gun and bulletproof vests to "Oklahoma bad men."

Locally, though, he was better known for sharing his bounty to help clothe and feed hungry friends and family members and picking up strangers' restaurant bills. His legend grew as hard-hearted bankers repeatedly took away homes and farms from people out of work or down on their luck. Another story had Floyd stealing banks' loan and mortgage records along with their cash.

At one point, the Oklahoma governor offered a reward for his capture. Floyd appealed on his own behalf—and to other downtrodden Okies. In a letter, he asked the governor to reconsider, saying, "I have robbed no one but the monied men."

The press, amused by his fancy clothes and slicked-back hair, always with a thin part, called him "Pretty Boy" Floyd. Everyone else called him Charley.

For a time in 1933, Floyd actually tried to retire and spent time baking fruit pies in his cousins' kitchens in small Oklahoma towns. But when some family members were arrested for harboring him, he stole a car and headed to Kansas City, Missouri, where he ended up in far more trouble than ever before.

The scene of the shooting at Kansas City's Union Station

The U.S. Bureau of Investigation, an investigative arm of the Department of Justice, had tracked down an escaped bank robber named Frank "Jelly" Nash in Hot Springs, Arkansas, and was returning him to prison in Leavenworth, Kansas. The agents who captured Nash took him by train to Kansas City's Union Station and were planning to drive him the thirty miles back to Leavenworth.

Unknown to the police and federal agents, word got out among Nash's tight-knit group of outlaw buddies that he would be transferred in Kansas City. A gunman was hired to free Nash. According to federal agents who later investigated the crime, Floyd needed cash and signed on to help out.

A little after 7 a.m. on June 17, 1933, the agents believed, Floyd, the gunman, and an associate were waiting with at least one submachine gun, and possibly more. A covey of officers—including two federal agents from Kansas City, two from Oklahoma City, a police chief from McAlester, Oklahoma, and two Kansas City cops—escorted Nash to the car.

After Nash was pushed into the front seat, the police heard someone call out, "Up! Up! Get your hands up!"

Perhaps out of nervousness, a bullet was fired from inside the car, likely killing Nash.

At the sound of the shot, another voice outside the car rang out: "Let 'em have it!"

A hailstorm of machine-gun bullets flew into the car. The two Kansas City police detectives were killed instantly, as were the Oklahoma police chief and a Kansas City federal agent. An Oklahoma federal agent was shot three times, while the Kansas City agent-in-charge was only grazed with a bullet. Just one man, an agent who bent forward in his seat when the shooting started, missed injury.

As the smoke lifted, the shooters jumped in a car and sped off. In maybe thirty seconds, it was over.

In the confusion of the moment, neither the police nor eyewitnesses were certain exactly what had happened. Were there two shooters? Three? Four? Were they skinny and tall or round and short? No one, it seemed, had gotten a good look. For months, the bureau and police would investigate a number of different suspects, including former bank robbers from several states. Though suspicion later settled on Floyd, he repeatedly denied to friends and family that he ever took part.

This was yet another slaughter, this time of law enforcement officers—cops and robbers on a grand scale. *Literary Digest* called it "The Machine-Gun Challenge to the Nation." In a matter of days, what became known as the Kansas City Massacre would set in motion permanent changes in the way the nation looked at and dealt with both the Tommy gun and crime.

The election of Franklin Delano Roosevelt as president in 1932 and the Democratic sweep that came with it ushered in a sea change in how politicians and Congress approached the Depression. Determined to turn the economy around, they proposed more federal programs than ever before, rather than relying on individual states or free market forces for solutions. Between March and June 1933, Congress passed and Roosevelt signed more than a dozen major new pieces of legislation aimed at saving homes, improving farm prices, protecting workers' rights, providing food to the hungry, and especially creating and providing jobs for millions of desperate, out-of-work Americans.

Within hours of the Kansas City debacle, the new government's

Attorney General Homer S. Cummings used the Union Station shooting and other crimes to push for expanded federal law enforcement and restrictions on Tommy guns.

attention would also shift to crime—the stickups, bank robberies, car thefts, and gun violence that had become a growing part of middle-American life since the mid-1920s.

By early July, Homer S. Cummings, Roosevelt's attorney general, was calling for aggressive government action. He wanted greater federal law enforcement powers so that criminals couldn't just move from state to state. And he raised a new idea: The nation, he said, needed "some method of preventing the lawless elements from getting machine guns and other firearms."

The Kansas City murders, Cummings said, were "a declaration of war by the underworld." The United States would respond full force with its own "war on crime."

On the surface, the U.S. government didn't have much with which to launch a war. Criminal laws and police were the business of states, cities, and towns. Few trusted—or wanted—the federal government to be involved. The Bureau of Investigation consisted of just a few hundred agents, with limited powers, in about two dozen offices across the country. (The agency wouldn't become the Federal Bureau of Investigation, or FBI, until 1935.)

But Roosevelt and Cummings did have one powerful weapon: the wily and hugely ambitious bulldog named John Edgar Hoover, the same man who had helped tail Irish gun-runners back in 1921. Hoover became director of the bureau in 1924 and had been working for more than a decade to make his employees professional and proper to a fault. He hired men who attended college, with a preference for lawyers and accountants. He demanded that his agents dress well, be punctual, avoid coffee breaks, and never drink alcohol, even outside the office. Professional appearance seemed more important to Hoover than skill.

In reality, his agents had few detective skills and almost no experience in tracking down criminals—but then they didn't do much of that. The laws in place then didn't allow bureau agents to carry guns or even make arrests like local police officers. But they did have experience in the evolving field of scientific crime analysis.

Since the early 1900s, the federal prison at Leavenworth had been collecting criminals' fingerprints. Shortly after Hoover took the reins at the bureau, he created an identification division, merging the Leavenworth fingerprint records with state and local records collected by the International Association of Chiefs of Police to create the first comprehensive set of prints. By the early 1930s, the collection had grown to about 3.8 million files.

In 1932, following the work of Chicago's Calvin Goddard, the bureau opened its first crime lab, specializing in handwriting and typewriter analysis. It would later add ballistics research and chemical analysis. By the time the war on crime was breaking out, the bureau was equipped to help identify criminals and their weapons.

Though Hoover publicly vowed to keep politicians from meddling

Bureau of Investigation fingerprint experts at work in 1932

with his agency or his men, he was also known to collect useful information for his bosses, especially the president of the United States. In a critical 1933 article, *Collier's* writer Ray Tucker charged that Hoover ran what was essentially a "secret federal police" force that at times had kept reports on U.S. senators, high-profile professors, and a Supreme Court judge. Hoover, Tucker noted, also had an "appetite for publicity" that was peculiar for a bureau "which, by the nature of its work, is supposed to operate in secrecy."

With Homer Cummings's declaration of war, Hoover had a perfect opportunity to use his skill at publicity to raise his own profile and that of his little bureau. Luckily for him, shortly after the devastating Kansas City Massacre, a career-building kidnapping case fell into his lap.

°₀ ° ₒ

Late on the night of July 22, 1933, a wealthy Oklahoma City oilman named Charles F. Urschel and his wife, Berenice, were playing one last bridge hand with friends when two men burst through their door. One wielded a Tommy gun, the other a pistol. Neither gunman knew which bridge player was Urschel. So they took both men at gunpoint.

By the time the friend was released outside of town, Berenice had called the Bureau of Investigation to report the abduction.

The kidnappers asked for a whopping $200,000 ransom—about $3.7 million in today's dollars—and the oil family was able to rustle it up. Nine days after Urschel was taken away at gunpoint, the oilman was released unharmed.

Oilman Charles Urschel at the trial of his kidnappers in October 1933

Under questioning, Urschel remembered many details about the shack where he had been held. He knew the car had crossed a long wooden bridge, likely a bridge into Texas. He had heard roosters crowing and pigs squealing. The water pump had a painful squeak and the water tasted bitterly of minerals. Perhaps most helpful, Urschel heard a plane fly overhead in the morning and early evening, except one day when it rained heavily. Investigators had a lot of information to go on.

But even more, the bureau had the good fortune to be chasing George "Machine Gun" Kelly and his wife, Kathryn. George was a bumbling, good-natured, and handsome rogue whom one author called, "probably the most inept of Depression-era criminals."

Born George F. Barnes, Kelly grew up in Memphis, the son of a

Mugshots of George "Machine Gun" Kelly and Kathryn Kelly, taken in 1933

middle-class insurance agent. In a rarity among criminals at the time, young Barnes had actually enrolled in college but dropped out after a semester. He had married, had two sons, and for a time, worked hard for his father-in-law. But when his mentor died in an industrial accident, he became a bootlegger. His wife divorced him.

At odds with his father, George dropped the Barnes name and took on Kelly, his mother's maiden name. In the late 1920s, he met the woman who would become his next wife and his partner in crime.

Kathryn Kelly was born Cleo Mae Brooks and had dropped out of school after eighth grade—but not before changing her first name to one she thought was more appealing. She married young, had a daughter, and then divorced. Another husband died with a gun and a typed note next to his body; his death was ruled a suicide.

Meeting at a Fort Worth speakeasy, the easygoing George and the ambitious and determined Kathryn hit it off. But their storybook romance was interrupted when George was sentenced to Leavenworth for bootlegging. There he got another education—in safecracking and bank robbery—and made friends with notorious criminals. He and Kathryn married when he got out in 1930, and George set about to become a professional crook. He told acquaintances he was in the "banking business."

Unfortunately for both of them, Kelly wasn't a natural. He got physically ill before bank jobs and was never especially fond of guns. But Kathryn liked clothes, fancy cars, and the fast life, and she pushed her husband to get better at it. She also liked to drink, and especially liked to brag when she was drinking. Along the way, she befriended some local police she thought might be helpful to her, including a Fort Worth, Texas, detective.

That detective began to suspect the Kellys from the moment he heard about the kidnapping. He alerted the federal bureau's Dallas office and repeatedly encouraged them to check out the home of Kathryn Kelly's mother near Paradise, Texas. When the rain patterns there matched Urschel's description, the bureau finally took notice.

By the time the bureau agents showed up in Paradise in early August, however, the Kellys were long gone, as was most of the money.

The couple hopscotched across the country to St. Paul, Minnesota; Cleveland; Chicago; Des Moines, Iowa; Mississippi; and Memphis, Tennessee. George dyed his hair bright yellow, and Kathryn picked up a red wig. Along the way, bureau agents narrowly missed them again and again, showing up just after they departed a relative's home or left for another city. In one instance, a Chicago agent named Melvin Purvis was told to stake out a tavern where the Kellys were receiving mail. He simply forgot to do it.

By now, newspapers were covering the search for Machine Gun Kelly. Where the nickname came from isn't completely clear. It may have just reflected that George carried a Tommy gun during the kidnapping. Later, though, J. Edgar Hoover would paint Kathryn as the shrewd, conniving brains behind the pair, the one who conceived the kidnapping and gave him the name.

Noting that Kathryn had bought a machine gun for George at a pawnshop, Hoover wrote: "[S]he rode into the country with him while he practiced to become an expert, finally reaching a point where he could knock a row of walnuts from the top of a fence and at a good distance. Meanwhile, Kathryn garnered the empty cartridges, to be kept for such times as she could hand them to friends, remarking:

" 'Here's a souvenir I brought you. It's a cartridge fired by George's machine gun—Machine-gun Kelly, you know.' "

There was likely some after-the-fact embellishment there. At the least, Kathryn's Texas home was in pecan country.

Even so, George's reputation—or Kathryn's boasting—was great enough that a federal agent sent a memo during the manhunt, noting, "Kelly is most proficient with a machine gun, it being said he can write his name with the bullets discharged from such a gun."

In late September, the bureau finally found George and Kathryn in a house in Memphis. As an agent crept into his room, Kelly told him, "I been waiting all night for you." And then he surrendered, without ever having fired a shot.

For years and years, J. Edgar Hoover told another story. In interviews, FBI-approved books, and movies, he said Kelly had shouted a plea: "Don't shoot, G-men!"

The bureau men had never heard the term for "government men," but, the legend goes, it stuck and later became a term of FBI bravery and daring.

Unfortunately, the story wasn't true. Many believe the "G-men" term originated with FBI publicity men trying to bolster their agency's reputation. But in an interview with the *Chicago American* after the Kellys' arrest, an agent attributed the phrase to Kathryn. She had sobbed when she was arrested and then put her arms around Kelly. "Honey, I guess it's all up for us," the agent quoted her as saying. "The 'g' men won't ever give us a break."

Hoover played the sensational crime and the sensational capture for all they were worth. In scrapbooks of news articles about the agency, now in the National Archives, several articles based on interviews with Hoover or his men detail the brilliant and clever detective work of his federal agents in meticulously tracking down the kidnappers—without mentioning any help from others or the bureau's mistakes. Blared one

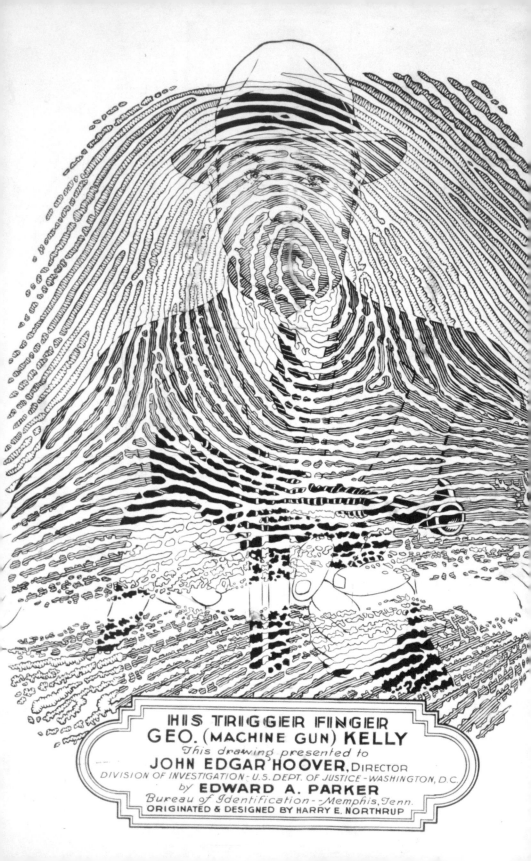

HIS TRIGGER FINGER
GEO. (MACHINE GUN) KELLY
This drawing presented to
JOHN EDGAR HOOVER, Director
DIVISION OF INVESTIGATION - U.S. DEPT. OF JUSTICE - WASHINGTON, D.C.
by
EDWARD A. PARKER
Bureau of Identification - Memphis, Tenn.
ORIGINATED & DESIGNED BY HARRY E. NORTHRUP

headline in the *Washington-Herald*: "The Urschel Kidnapers' Mistake: They Forgot There Was a Justice Department and a Hoover."

Kathryn Kelly tried to blame everything on her husband, but to no avail. She and George both received life sentences. When the government, as part of its crackdown on crime, opened the maximum-security prison on Alcatraz Island, in San Francisco Bay, Machine Gun Kelly would join Al Capone there.

The war on crime itself was just beginning. A hotheaded crook with a quick trigger finger named Lester Gillis—better known as Baby Face Nelson—was robbing banks. Clyde Barrow and his partner Bonnie Parker were holding up stores and crisscrossing the Southwest. And the most notorious Depression-era bandit of all, John Dillinger, was just getting going.

A cartoon given to J. Edgar Hoover commemorated his agency's work in capturing Machine Gun Kelly.

CHAPTER 11
COPS AND ROBBERS

WHEN AL CAPONE WANTED powerful guns, he purchased them. But the Depression-era bandits saw an easier and cheaper way: They simply robbed police stations and state National Guard armories, picking up their arms courtesy of taxpayers.

In the summer and fall of 1933, that was the main way a little-known parolee named John Dillinger and his gang got the guns they would use to keep law enforcement mostly at bay.

Dillinger, thirty years old, had a rough background. His mother had died when he was three and he never took to school, becoming increasingly rebellious as a teen. As a young man, he had robbed and injured a grocer in his hometown of Mooresville, Indiana, ultimately serving more than eight years in a reformatory for young men and then a prison for hardened criminals.

During his long prison time, he formed close friendships with bank robbers and other crooks who filled him with tales of riches, fun, and

An early mugshot of John Dillinger

pretty women on the outside. When he was finally paroled in May 1933, Dillinger promised to help his buddies get out as well.

Almost immediately, the man with a crooked smile and a movie star's dimpled chin set out on a bank-robbing spree through Indiana, Ohio, and northern Kentucky to raise money to buy arms. Cool and cocky, he would athletically leap railings and counters to get to the cash. In September 1933, true to his word, he managed to secretly deliver pistols to his friends that would allow them to break out of prison.

Then, taking a break, Dillinger headed to Dayton, Ohio, to visit a woman he was romancing.

He had hardly arrived when police surrounded him. A clever Indiana state trooper, intrigued with Dillinger's leaping skill, had been tracking his work—and his girlfriend.

By the time Dillinger's old gang was free, he was locked up in a jail cell in Lima, Ohio, awaiting trial for a bank raid. But his prison friends turned out to be just as loyal to him as he had been to them. On October 12, three men in suits barged into the office of the Lima jail. "We're Michigan officers and we would like to see John Dillinger," one of them told the sheriff, Jess Sarber.

"Let me see your credentials," the sheriff replied.

The man pulled a pistol, and when the sheriff moved to pick up a gun, the visitor fired right into him. The other men forced a deputy to open the cell. Dillinger grabbed a hat and coat and was whisked away.

Sheriff Sarber died a few hours later.

The breakout would make news coast to coast, marking the first time the name Dillinger widely appeared outside the Midwest. It was also the beginning of one of the most violent, daring, and closely watched crime sprees the United States would ever see—and the beginning of the end of the Tommy gun's reign as a crime weapon.

In the week after the jailbreak, the men went "shopping" for guns, ammunition, and money. They stopped in the Auburn, Indiana, police station and emptied the gun cabinet of a Tommy gun, some pistols and rifles, ammunition, and bulletproof vests. A few days later, by one account, they relieved the Peru, Indiana, City Hall of another Tommy gun, two sawed-off shotguns, and more bulletproofs vests. They finished the week by removing $75,000 from a bank in Greencastle, Indiana, a significant haul equal to about $1.4 million today.

Their spree set off a storm among Indiana police. The governor provided $10,000 for machine guns, ten squad cars, and bulletproof vests. He also asked Hoover and the Bureau of Investigation for assistance in

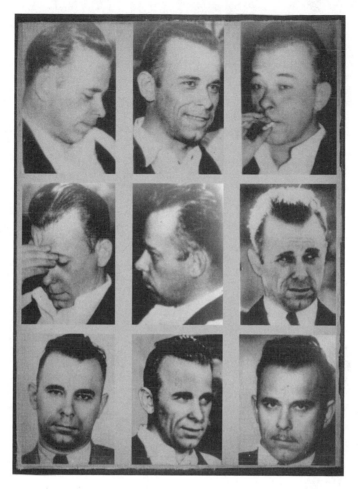

Authorities collected many faces of John Dillinger—but had trouble catching him.

tracking Dillinger. But Hoover, knowing his agents weren't very good at manhunts, offered help with only fingerprints.

Instead, the state assigned some 2,000 National Guard soldiers, state police, and volunteers from the American Legion to patrol the state's roads, looking for "the desperados who have been terrorizing Indiana and surrounding states for more than a month." Police were so on edge that an official warned people celebrating Halloween to take care not to be confused with the dangerous gang.

Following page: Armed Indiana police stop a car in search of Dillinger gang members in fall 1933.

Evelyn "Billie" Frechette
in May 1934

While Indiana was mobilizing, however, Dillinger and his gang were settling down in Chicago. Dillinger was dating Evelyn "Billie" Frechette, a twenty-six-year-old who had grown up on the Menominee Reservation in Wisconsin and had been running the hatcheck at a nightclub.

The men rented nice apartments, purchased new suits and coats, went to the dentist, and started their evenings at the movies. Dillinger loved seeing the picture shows, especially since sound had been added to movies in the late 1920s, while he was in prison. Afterward, the group might go to a restaurant or club. They broke their routine only to rob a bank with a Thompson gun in tow.

Despite the gang's lower profile, the Chicago police were looking for them. In mid-November, three cars of well-armed police tried to catch Dillinger as he left a doctor's office, but he managed to outdrive them. The next month, a Dillinger gang member killed a city detective who tried to corner him at an auto-repair shop, putting the gang in the headlines again.

In response to the shooting, the Chicago police created a fifty-member Dillinger Squad that was to spend every minute stalking the increasingly dangerous criminals.

Quietly, the gang slipped out of town. Some of them dyed their hair dark brown. Dillinger dyed his red and began to grow a mustache.

The group would soon gather in Daytona Beach, Florida, for a little vacation and to ring in the New Year. The visit was unusually uneventful, without any robberies or police run-ins. Most of the gang members had never seen a beach before, and no one suspected who they were.

As the new year began, the war on crime was still a work in progress. Hoover and his men still didn't know who had opened fire on law enforcement officers at Kansas City's Union Station, and they were relieved to leave the Dillinger gang to local police. Hoover's boss, Homer Cummings, hadn't yet introduced his plans for cutting crime.

Though some steps had been taken to ease the national suffering from the Depression, true recovery was a long way off and cynicism simmered under the surface. Many people had lost their savings when banks failed, and others were still losing their houses and farms when banks called in their loans. Meanwhile, mining and steel companies were increasingly intimidating workers who wanted to unionize.

Government hearings into the stock market crash that preceded the Depression had uncovered all kinds of questionable behavior by the nation's bank leaders and top finance people. Inappropriate investments had been pushed on unsuspecting customers, and executives had enriched themselves even as depositors and investors lost their savings. Amid all those revelations, many citizens found themselves rooting for the Dillinger gang against bankers, police, and politicians who they felt had made their lives harder.

During his State of the Union speech to Congress on January 4, 1934, President Roosevelt painted both the bankers and the bank robbers with the same brush. He criticized the "unethical" behavior of top business officials and the "criminal" behavior of "organized banditry," and he promised reforms. "These violations of ethics and these violations of law call on the strong arm of government for their immediate suppression," he said.

Before too long, Congress would be considering laws to overhaul the financial markets, along with bills from the Justice Department and Homer Cummings to fight crime. Those proposals would make it a federal offense to assault a federal agent, rob a national bank, or transport stolen goods of $5,000 or more across state lines. Though it got less attention, Cummings also asked for the most comprehensive gun law ever considered, one that would require registration of all machine guns, pistols, and rifles.

In mid-January, Dillinger and another gang member returned to Chicago. Foolishly, they decided to hit up a bank while they were there.

Without their usual comrades and their careful planning, the heist went badly. Dillinger uncharacteristically lost his cool and turned his Tommy gun on a police officer, killing a father of three with eight bullets to the chest. It was, by all accounts, his first murder, and it unsettled him.

He made a getaway, but the murder raised the stakes.

Shortly after, Dillinger and Frechette headed to Tucson, Arizona, to meet up with the rest of the gang. Their stay there might have gone unnoticed had there not been a small fire in one of the hotels. Two of the gang members tried to get to their rooms to rescue their luggage. When a firefighter helped them retrieve it, they gave him a generous tip.

A few days later, the firefighter happened to be reading a crime magazine when he recognized one of the men whose luggage he had rescued. Later, bellboys at the hotel remembered how heavy the luggage had been—reflecting the guns and ammunition stuffed inside.

Tucson police were called. They searched through "wanted" posters to identify the men. One by one, they arrested each of them without a shot being fired. Dillinger was stopped on his way into a house by a detective who already had his pistol out.

Altogether, four men and three women were held at the Pima County jail under heavy guard. Six Tommy guns had been seized, along with more than $30,000 in cash. This time, it seemed, Dillinger's luck had finally run out.

A few days later, Dillinger was on his first plane ride, heading to Chicago to stand trial for murder.

While John Dillinger was held at Crown Point, Indiana, guards provided extra security.

Though Dillinger was a slight man, just five feet, seven inches tall, the Chicago police brought out a force capable of destroying a small platoon to meet him. The Dillinger Squad was there, accompanied by other Chicago lawmen and police from nearby towns—more than a hundred cops by one count. Several hundred onlookers watched as he was pushed into a car, wearing only a blue suit and shivering without a coat or hat. Then a long caravan of police cars, carrying at least six Tommy guns, several dozen pistols, and assorted rifles and shotguns, escorted Dillinger to a jail that was supposed to be escape-proof.

On the plane he had given an interview, saying he didn't smoke much and he hardly drank. "My only bad habit, I guess, is robbing banks," he said. He denied having murdered anyone. He mentioned his father and brother in Indiana and admitted, "I guess they ain't very proud of me."

He arrived at the Crown Point, Indiana, jail that evening to a scrum of reporters and photographers. "Are you glad to see Indiana again?" a reporter asked.

"About as glad as Indiana is to see me," Dillinger replied.

He painted himself as an "unfortunate boy" who got drunk, made a mistake, and went to prison. There, he said, he met some "good fellas" and decided he wanted to help them. So he helped them break out. "I stick to my friends and they stick to me," he said.

Calm, charismatic, and well spoken, Dillinger looked and acted like a regular guy. His legend grew even more.

During the impromptu press conference, a photographer called out for the prosecutor standing next to Dillinger to put his arm around him. Caught in the moment, the prosecutor complied. Dillinger, playing the scene for all it was worth, propped his elbow on the man's shoulder as if they were old friends. To those who saw the photograph across the country the next day, it looked as if Dillinger was hanging out with old acquaintances. It was an image the Indiana officials would come to deeply regret.

Looking as though he's among friends, John Dillinger props his elbow on the shoulder of prosecutor Robert Estill, who stands next to Sheriff Lillian Holley.

Dillinger's trial initially was set for February, but his lawyer got an extension until mid-March. He was kept in a new, second-floor part of the jail, with several locked doors and several armed guards between him and freedom. The jail had even added volunteers and National Guardsmen for extra support.

On a cold and rainy March 3, the door to his cell area was unlocked for morning cleanup. Dillinger had a crazy, harebrained scheme—and nothing to lose.

Using a wooden gun with a brass barrel that was painted to look real, he was able to lock several key jail officials in the second-floor cell. (Initial reports said Dillinger had developed a hobby of whittling and had whittled the gun himself. In truth, the wooden gun probably was smuggled to him.)

Dillinger teamed up with another prisoner, Herbert Youngblood, and the two made their way downstairs, where they snatched two submachine guns from an office. Once they were well armed, they easily navigated the rest of the jail and slipped undetected out a back door.

In a nearby garage, Dillinger forced a mechanic to give up a V-8 Ford, which turned out to be the sheriff's car. Once on the road, Dillinger made his way back to Chicago.

Later, Dillinger would brag to his sister in a letter, "I locked eight deputys and a dozen trustys up with my wooden gun before I got my hands on the two machine guns and you should have seen their faces. Ha! Ha! Ha! Pulling that off was worth ten years of my life! Ha! Ha!"

His cockiness was earned. The *New York Times* called it "a daring escape that rivals the exploits of the heroes of Wild West thrillers."

The remarkable headlines also finally persuaded J. Edgar Hoover to join the chase. Dillinger hadn't actually broken a federal law until he took the sheriff's car across state lines. Hoover's men now had good reasons to make the notorious bank robber the poster boy of their war on crime.

It would make John Dillinger the most hunted man in America.

CHAPTER 12
PUBLIC ENEMIES

MANY, MANY MILES AWAY from John Dillinger, Attorney General Homer Cummings and President Roosevelt were trying to push their crime bills through Congress.

In March, Cummings told the Senate Judiciary Committee that the federal government needed new legal powers to halt a criminal underworld "that has more people under arms than in the army and navy of the United States."

Asked a senator from Indiana: Would the proposed legislation allow the government to stop John Dillinger?

Yes, Cummings told him, because one bill would make it illegal for a criminal to move from one state to another to avoid prosecution.

In late March, the Senate passed seven bills after Senate leaders were told that President Roosevelt wanted the measures approved quickly. Another bill, to impose new restrictions on machine guns and other weapons, was still in the works.

The proposed laws would give the Bureau of Investigation the authority to make arrests. J. Edgar Hoover promised that his people were ready to move "on a minute's notice." Ignoring his department's small staff and still-limited skills, he said confidently: "Our men are ready. They will not require additional training."

But Cummings's plan hit a big snag with the House of Representatives. Hatton Sumners, a former Texas prosecutor, chaired the House Judiciary Committee, and he wasn't impressed with Cummings's bills. He felt some of them were badly drafted and others took too much power away from local authorities and gave too much to the federal government. He refused to let the bills out of his committee in their present form.

At a cabinet meeting on March 23, Cummings asked President Roosevelt to contact Representative Sumners "and try to get him to take a more friendly attitude toward our pending crime bills."

Representative Hatton Sumners of Texas

The president was headed out on vacation soon, and his phone call with Sumners didn't turn out to be very friendly. Roosevelt asked when the crime bills would be sent to the full House for consideration. Sumners replied "that he did not think they ought to be reported," at least not as they had been submitted.

Angry, Roosevelt responded, "How would you like to have your committee taken away from you?"

"I'd just like to see anybody try," Sumners shot back, and then ended the conversation. The bills remained stuck in the House committee.

○ ○ ○ ○

Never one to dawdle for long, John Dillinger quickly made new contacts, joining up with one of the Depression-era's most violent men, Lester Gillis.

Lester Gillis was publicly known as Baby Face Nelson.

Gillis was a small man, just five feet, four inches tall, and, at twenty-five, younger than most of Dillinger's pals. Like many of the crooks of the era, he had started out stealing cars and graduated to robbing banks. In 1930, in trouble again, he had adopted the name "George Nelson." Later that year, he and two others brazenly mugged the wife of Chicago's mayor on a city street, stealing her jewelry. Mary Walker Thompson told a reporter her attacker "had a baby face. He was good looking, hardly more than a boy . . ." The press began to call him Baby Face Nelson—but no one dared use that nickname to his face.

In the weeks after the Crown Point escape, Dillinger, Nelson, and their new gang robbed banks in Sioux Falls, South Dakota, and Mason City, Iowa, where Dillinger was wounded in the shoulder. He and Frechette set up an apartment in a fancy St. Paul, Minnesota, neighborhood to recuperate.

Before long, however, a Hoover agent and a police officer were knocking on their door, following a tip that a criminal might be inside. Dillinger and Frechette escaped out a rear door, letting loose a burst of machine-gun fire. A few hours later, after finding machine guns and photos in the apartment, the officers discovered that the man who got away was Dillinger.

In Washington, Hoover was furious about the "atrocious bungling" of the raid. He was mad that Dillinger had fired on his agent. He was angry that his agent hadn't brought a machine gun—and irate that he wasn't told about the raid in advance. In his frustration, he declared that capturing Dillinger would become his bureau's highest priority.

Unfortunately, his men were so inexperienced and overwhelmed that they repeatedly arrived just after Dillinger had left a place.

From St. Paul, Dillinger stopped briefly in Chicago and then headed

On a quick trip to his family's Indiana home, Dillinger posed with his fake wooden gun and a Tommy gun.

to his family's place in Mooresville, Indiana, for a reunion and dinner. There he posed for pictures with his wooden gun and a Tommy gun. The bureau hadn't thought to have someone stake out the family home. And two agents sent from out of town to keep an eye on the family drove right past Dillinger on a local road without recognizing him.

Back in Chicago, agents finally managed to arrest Frechette at a tavern. But they neglected to notice that Dillinger himself was sitting in a car parked outside. (Frechette would later be sentenced to prison time.)

Agents would soon get another chance—one that seemed like a slam dunk.

In search of a break and a little quiet in late April, Dillinger, Nelson, and the new gang decided to trek 400 miles north to a lodge and tavern known as Little Bohemia, near Mercer, Wisconsin.

After a steak dinner, the men sat down for a friendly game of cards. The lodge operator noticed gun holsters under their coats. He found a newspaper and confirmed his worst fear: Dillinger was in his lodge.

The owner pulled Dillinger aside to say he knew who he was. Dillinger tried to reassure him. "All we want is to eat and rest for a few days," he said. "We'll pay you well and get out. There won't be no trouble."

Still uncomfortable, the lodge owner smuggled a note out in a pack of cigarettes, asking that federal agents be notified.

Melvin Purvis, the Chicago agent who had forgotten about Machine Gun Kelly and whose men had missed Dillinger several times already, took the call. He alerted Hoover in Washington, and a team of about twenty federal agents prepared to head to Wisconsin. Four men came in a car, while others came in chartered planes from St. Paul and Chicago. Time was crucial: The Dillinger gang was expected to leave the next day.

In Washington, Hoover was so sure that Dillinger would be caught that he told reporters to be ready for big news.

But in their scramble to get to Wisconsin, the agents had neglected to put together a detailed attack plan. They were well armed with Tommy guns but ill prepared. As they drove up to the lodge in the dark, dogs started barking. And at the worst possible time, three local men who had been drinking at the bar left the lodge and climbed into a car. Though the agents ordered the men to halt, the men didn't hear them over the loud car radio.

The agents opened fire.

In the noise and confusion of car doors and gunfire, Dillinger and other gang members inside the lodge quickly realized that police had arrived. After sending a spray of machine-gun fire toward the agents below, they jumped out a second-floor window into a huge mound of snow and slid down a bank. Out of sight, they made their way around the lake that bordered the property.

Dillinger and two others were able to commandeer a car and hit the road. Baby Face Nelson, who had been staying in a nearby cabin, headed in a different direction. Trying to hijack yet another auto, he came across a car with government agents and angrily opened fire on them with his Tommy gun. Then he stole their car.

The federal raid that had started with such promise had dissolved into a total disaster. Soon, it would be a national scandal. Locals laughed at what they called the "bungle of the revenooers," a jab at the income-tax-collecting federal government. Bullet holes marked the lodge and windows were broken out, but the only people left to arrest were three women who had accompanied the gang. Yet another arsenal was left behind: six Tommy guns, a dozen shotguns and rifles, and a large quantity of ammunition.

One innocent local man was dead and two others were injured, shot by federal agents. One federal agent was dead, and a second agent and a local constable were injured, shot by Nelson. On top of that, Dillinger and Nelson had gotten away.

The Dillinger gang left behind an arsenal, including Tommy guns.

CHAPTER 13

RECOIL

SOMEHOW, SOME WAY, the Roosevelt administration was able to turn a disaster into an opportunity.

Even as the ugly and messy details of the Little Bohemia affair were still streaming out of Wisconsin, President Roosevelt again called on Congress to finally approve his crime bills. This time, Representative Hatton Sumners listened. (He also made a point of denying reports that the president had summoned him to the White House; rather, he insisted, the topic came up while he was already there.)

Sumners promised that his House Judiciary Committee would take up the bills right away, even though he still believed the legislation trounced on states' rights.

"Public opinion demands action," he said the next day, after his committee approved two bills, one that prohibited fleeing to another state to avoid prosecution and another that made it a federal crime to take stolen property across state lines.

"A wrath like that which kindled the frontier when the vigilantes chased out the gunmen is sweeping America," he added. Personally, he said, he would prefer citizens clean up their own communities and get rid of corrupt local officials and courts. "But now they demand swift and efficient action by the federal government to down crime and erase the criminal, and will get it.

"These laws will smash the criminal gangs and make another Dillinger impossible."

Perhaps to deflect attention from the agents' mistakes at Little Bohemia, Homer Cummings made the somewhat absurd statement that the government could have avoided the tragedy in Wisconsin with an armored car. He called for faster cars, a few armored cars, airplanes, and at least 200 more men to assist the 400 special agents already working for Hoover. To have enough Tommy guns, the Justice Department already had dismantled an exhibit of machine guns taken from gangsters and distributed them to its men. Cummings would ask Congress for more money for the federal police force.

Even while Washington was trying to add more teeth to crime efforts, the government found itself losing ground in the publicity war to Dillinger. A sixteen-year-old Boy Scout who was "governor for an hour" in Indiana was asked what he thought of Dillinger. The young man answered, "I'm for him," explaining later that he was "always for the underdog." *Detective* magazine reported that Dillinger newsreels in the movie theaters were drawing more applause than Roosevelt.

On May 18, Roosevelt signed six new crime bills into law, assuring the public that the federal government would crack down on interstate crime. But he also asked for support from citizens—and scolded them for siding with crooks. "Law enforcement and gangster extermination

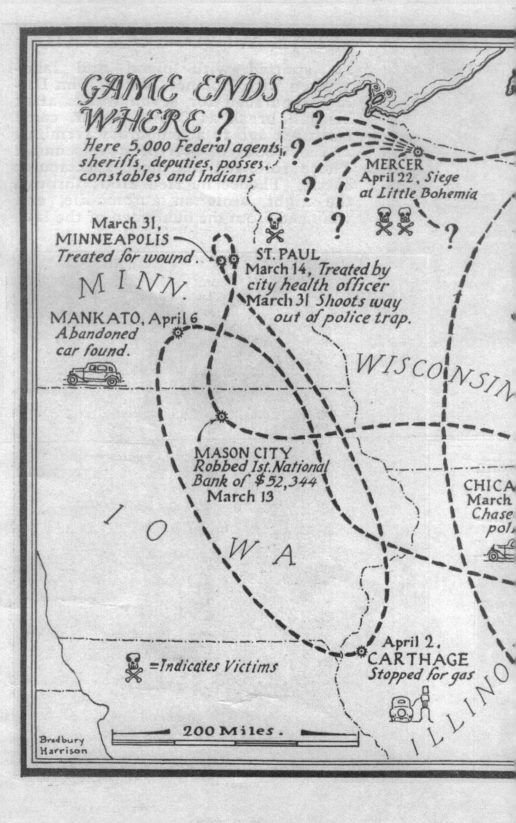

GAME ENDS WHERE ?

Here 5,000 Federal agents, sheriffs, deputies, posses, constables and Indians

MERCER April 22, Siege at Little Bohemia

March 31, **MINNEAPOLIS** Treated for wound.

ST. PAUL March 14, Treated by city health officer March 31 Shoots way out of police trap.

MINN.

MANKATO, April 6 Abandoned car found.

WISCONSIN

MASON CITY Robbed 1st. National Bank of $52,344 March 13

IOWA

CHICA March Chase pol.

= Indicates Victims

April 2, **CARTHAGE** Stopped for gas

ILLINO

200 Miles.

Bradbury Harrison

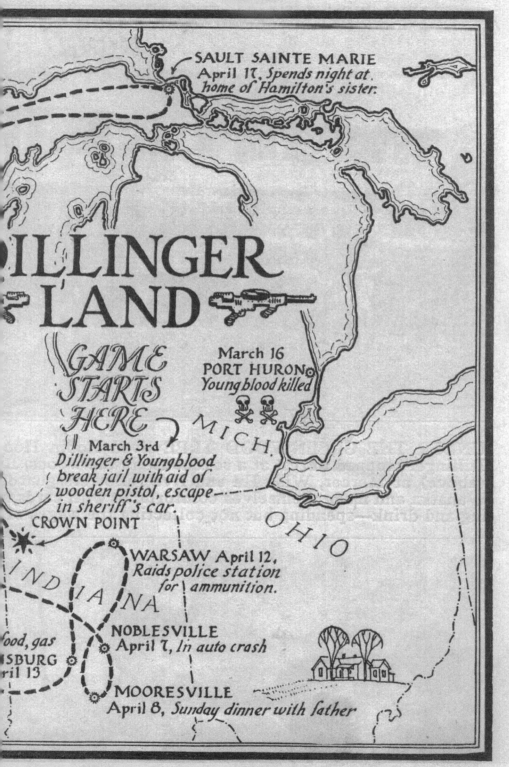

SAULT SAINTE MARIE
April 17, Spends night at
home of Hamilton's sister.

DILLINGER
LAND

*GAME
STARTS
HERE*

March 16
PORT HURON
Young blood killed

March 3rd
*Dillinger & Youngblood
break jail with aid of
wooden pistol, escape
in sheriff's car.*
CROWN POINT

M I C H.

O H I O

I N D I A N A

WARSAW April 12,
*Raids police station
for ammunition.*

...ood, gas
...SBURG
...ril 13

NOBLESVILLE
April 7, *In auto crash*

MOORESVILLE
April 8, *Sunday dinner with father*

Time magazine mapped out Dillinger's travels after the Crown Point escape, making his
activity seem like an entertaining cat-and-mouse game with law enforcement.

President Roosevelt signs six crime bills in May 1934, while (left to right) Homer Cummings, J. Edgar Hoover, Senator Henry Ashurst, and Assistant Attorney General Joseph Keenan look on.

cannot be made completely effective so long as a substantial part of the public looks with tolerance upon known criminals, permits public officers to be corrupted or intimidated by them, or applauds efforts to romanticize crime," he said.

"Federal men are constantly facing machine-gun fire in the pursuit of gangsters. I ask citizens, individually and as organized groups, to recognize the facts and meet them with courage and determination."

Despite the new laws, Cummings's number one crime bill—designed to keep deadly weapons out of the hands of criminals—was still pending. It faced a significant hurdle. For months, Cummings had been fighting to restrict Tommy guns and easily concealed weapons, such as pistols and revolvers, with what was nicknamed the Anti–Machine Gun bill.

But this bill, unlike the others, had stiff public opposition. Makers of firearms, sportsmen's organizations, and other opponents, "looking to the safeguarding of their legitimate interests," were conferring with officials, the *New York Times* reported. Though the fight would largely take place out of the public eye, this bill would be much harder to pass.

From the very start of his plan to regulate guns, Homer Cummings and his Justice Department had to consider a potential obstacle: the U.S. Constitution.

Except for the law banning mail-order sales of handguns in 1927, the federal government itself had never passed a gun-control law in the nation's history. The Justice Department looked at other federal laws that the U.S. Supreme Court had found to be allowed under the Constitution. Though it didn't cite it specifically, it also apparently studied the Second Amendment.

The amendment is poorly worded, grammatically challenging, and at best, confusing. In other words, it is ripe for many interpretations.

In June 1789, about a year after the new country had ratified the Constitution, James Madison proposed to the House of Representatives a list of rights the new Americans should have. In addition to the rights of free speech and freedom of religion, the right to a jury and a speedy trial, he proposed this:

"The right of the people to keep and bear arms shall not be infringed; a well armed, and well regulated militia being the best security of a free country: but no person religiously scrupulous of bearing arms, shall be compelled to render military service in person."

The House debated the amendment, focusing on a huge issue in

James Madison initially offered seventeen amendments to the new Constitution. Ultimately, only ten were adopted.

the newly formed government: Would the states or the new federal government be in control? Having just fought off an oppressive government, the legislators didn't want to create another one. Some kind of military defense was surely needed, but how much of one and what kind?

In working through the language, the House turned the wording around to put the militia first. It also kept in an exemption for Quakers and other pacifists, who might refuse to take part in military action. It sent this version to the Senate:

"A well regulated militia, composed of the body of the People, being the best security of a free State, the right of the people to keep and bear arms, shall not be infringed, but no one religiously scrupulous of bearing arms, shall be compelled to render military service in person."

The religious clause turned out to be controversial and the Senate deleted it. It then tightened the wording further, and this became the Second Amendment to the Constitution:

"A well regulated Militia, being necessary to the security of a free State, the right of the people to keep and bear Arms, shall not be infringed."

Apparently, no English teachers were around to protest the wording.

After adopting the Bill of Rights in late 1791, Congress then followed with a law requiring many men to own guns. The Uniform Militia Act called on "every free, able-bodied white male citizen" between the ages of eighteen and forty-five to be a part of the nation's new militia. Those men were (in theory, at least) required to own their own muskets or firelocks and supply ammunition to help support the country.

Women, slaves, freed blacks, and Native Americans were prohibited from serving, reflecting deep-rooted prejudices and the concerns of colonial white men about whether those groups should own firearms.

Over time, the United States developed a strong national military, and within a century, those militias had lost their relevance. They were replaced in the early 1900s with state National Guards, which are trained by the federal government and serve both their states and the nation.

The presence of the Second Amendment didn't keep states and local governments from adopting laws restricting guns. As revolvers and pistols became more common, citizens grew concerned about weapons that could be easily concealed in pockets and coats, and about unnecessary violence in their communities. Local governments passed ordinances requiring visitors to check their guns at the town limits, though the laws weren't always enforced.

In the West, in particular, even women and small children learned to use handguns for protection at home and on their property. But there were also laws prohibiting the carrying of firearms, though rifles and shotguns often were excluded. In the 1850s, Galveston, Texas, could impose a fine of $5 on anyone firing a gun within city limits and up to $100—a significant amount—for carrying concealed weapons. As early as the 1870s, Texas could levy a fine of $50 to $500 for carrying a handgun to a school, church, or party. In 1871, Denver could impose a fine of at least $50 for carrying a concealed weapon. In the 1880s and 1890s, cattlemen led efforts to ban pistols at ranches and during roundups to cut down on violence and crime.

In fact, one of the most famous shoot-outs of all time, the 1881 gun-fight at the O.K. Corral in Tombstone, Arizona, started because some cowboys refused to check their firearms and defied local laws by wearing them. When the shooting stopped, three men were dead and three were wounded.

After the Civil War, blacks across the nation had the right to carry guns, and in the South, some joined militias. In response, some Southern states passed "Black Codes," laws intended to take away the freed men's freedoms, including gun ownership. Racist groups such as the Ku Klux Klan viciously attacked blacks throughout the South in an often-successful attempt to disarm them.

From the time the Bill of Rights was adopted until the 1930s, none of the handful of gun lawsuits that made their way to the U.S. Supreme Court addressed whether the Second Amendment gave individuals a right to own firearms. From the earliest days, settlers had restricted some gun ownership, for instance, by trying to stop firearms trading with Native Americans and forbidding slaves to have guns. Such

Blacks gather their dead after the Colfax Massacre in Louisiana, a vicious incident in which white supremacists attacked a black militia, murdering up to 150 black men.

efforts, including the disarming of blacks during Reconstruction, underscored a reality throughout American history: Those with guns held political power and those without firearms clearly did not.

By the time Homer Cummings was trying to disarm gangsters and bandits in the 1930s, local laws requiring gun permits, such as New York's Sullivan law, had been around for two decades. In considering how to effectively restrict criminal use of guns, Cummings knew the federal government might not be able to legally ban a specific weapon. So he settled on two powers that he was certain the federal government had: He could require owners to register guns and he could tax the sale of them. Neither of those would keep someone from owning a gun.

Since the mid-1920s, the National Rifle Association of America had been on an expansion streak. Under the direction of its top executive, Milton A. Reckord, a World War I veteran and a businessman, it expanded its police-training program, took over a junior rifle corps for young people, and promoted its competitions. In 1929, to get more news to its members, it started a publicity bureau. By 1934, it had about 33,000 individual members, who paid $3 a year, up from about 15,000 in 1924, and it had 2,200 shooting clubs, with ten to several hundred members each. Altogether, it claimed about 250,000 members.

In early 1934, up to a dozen bills dealing with firearms were pending in Congress. The long deadlines of its *American Rifleman* magazine made it impossible for the NRA keep its members up to date on the latest developments. So it created its first legislative arm to alert members and urge them to bombard Congress with responses.

(The NRA already was at odds with the Roosevelt administration. One of the president's key New Deal programs, the National Industrial Recovery Act, leased space in the same building as the NRA, and then adopted a logo abbreviating its initials to NRA. Mail was routinely delivered to the wrong offices, and confusion reigned until the Supreme Court voided the government's program in 1935.)

Reckord and then-NRA President Karl Frederick, a former Olympic shooting champion, especially were unhappy with a provision in Cummings's bill that would require individuals to be fingerprinted when they bought a pistol or handgun and to register those weapons.

The Justice Department had singled out concealable weapons because far more criminals were using small weapons than machine guns, rifles, or shotguns, with similar deadly results. In 1932, about 7,500 Americans were murdered with firearms, and about 8,000 people

Milton A. Reckord, the top executive at the National Rifle Association, helped expand the group's membership and reach.

committed suicide with them—with the vast majority of those deaths coming from handguns.

In an urgent letter to members, the NRA argued that if pistols and revolvers were included, rifles and shotguns would be next. "Once on the books," it wrote, "the Attorney General can then go to the next Congress and say, 'the firearms law we have needs a slight amendment.'"

Then, it warned, within a year, "every rifle and shotgun owner in the country will find himself paying a special revenue tax and having himself fingerprinted and photographed for the Federal 'rogues' gallery' every time he buys or sells a gun of any description."

Letters, calls, and telegrams poured into Congress opposing the bill.

Despite their strong stance on handguns, both Reckord and Frederick supported the government's efforts to register machine guns and sawed-off shotguns. "You can be just as severe with machines guns and sawed-off shotguns as you desire, and we will go along with you," Reckord said.

155

Initially, the bill defined a machine gun as a weapon that could fire twelve shots or more without reloading. But the pair pointed out that many guns had magazines allowing them to load and fire twelve or more bullets. Rather, they convinced legislators, a machine gun should be defined as one that could automatically empty a magazine with one pull of the trigger—what we call automatic weapons today.

In their testimony before both the House and the Senate, neither man brought up the Second Amendment. When asked specifically about it, Frederick said he believed the federal government could impose taxes on firearms. But the pair made clear that registering handguns wasn't going to be acceptable to them—even after a member of the House Ways and Means Committee pointed out that drivers needed licenses and cars had to be registered.

Answered Frederick: "Automobiles are a much more essential instrument of crime than pistols. Any police officer will tell you that. They are much more dangerous to ordinary life, because they kill approximately 30,000 people a year."

In a nutshell, wrote the *Christian Science Monitor,* one of the very few newspapers to cover the battle, the Justice Department and the NRA just weren't going to see eye to eye:

"Is it too much to ask of Mr. John Smith, citizen, to go to the trouble of registering his weapon—including fingerprinting—if he wants to own one, in order to combat growing depredations of Bill Jones, gangster?" it wrote.

"To this question, the Department of Justice says, 'No!'

"The National Rifle Association says, 'Yes!' "

The Justice Department called the NRA "selfish" and tried to argue that registering a handgun was a small price to pay for putting an end to so much violent crime. It acknowledged that criminals wouldn't register their guns—and that maybe honest individuals wouldn't, either—but adding the requirement would give it another way to quickly charge and convict criminals who carried guns without the proper paperwork.

Ultimately, Congress sided with the NRA, the American Legion, and others, stripping out all references to pistols and revolvers.

The government made one last appeal, to the General Federation of Women's Clubs, which represented about two million women nationwide. In late May, the women urged their members to contact their representatives and demand that they put the provision back.

A 1934 banquet of the General Federation of Women's Clubs

Perhaps, said one club official, if NRA members were strong enough to change the bill, "two million American club-women are strong enough to lick them to a frazzle and make them put back into that measure the pistols and revolvers they deleted from it."

Legislators didn't budge. On June 26, 1934, just before adjourning its session, Congress passed the National Firearms Act, putting a hefty $200 tax on the purchase of a Tommy gun or other automatic weapon— essentially doubling the price. Dealers who sold the guns would have to pay an annual $200 fee. The law also required buyers and owners of machine guns and sawed-off shotguns to register their weapons and be fingerprinted.

It wasn't what Homer Cummings had wanted, but it was a start, an effort to take the Tommy gun, the most deadly weapon of all, off the street.

Now, something still had to be done about John Dillinger.

CHAPTER 14

RELOAD

ULTIMATELY, **JOHN DILLINGER'S** appetite for
women led to his downfall—but not before he took an exceptionally
bold move to avoid capture.

Around the time that Dillinger's escapades were helping push the
National Firearms Act through Congress, the bandit arranged for a
doctor to rearrange his very famous face. In late May, in the back bedroom of a liquor-seller's home, two doctors prepared to fill in his most
distinguishing characteristic, his dimpled chin.

The operation got off to a rough start. The assistant gave Dillinger too much anesthetic. The gangster swallowed his tongue and
stopped breathing. As Dillinger turned blue, the other doctor grabbed
forceps to retrieve his tongue and then revived him. Once their patient was breathing again, they removed three moles between his
eyes and took skin from his jaw to fill in his chin. Then they tightened up his cheeks.

As John Dillinger turned thirty-one, the government took the unusual step of offering a financial reward for information leading to his capture.

A week later, they touched up their work, filling in more of the dimple and applying an acid to his fingers that was intended to change his fingerprints.

In late June, as Dillinger was turning thirty-one years old, the FBI stepped up its pursuit, naming him its Public Enemy No. 1, the most wanted man in America. With money approved by Congress, it offered $10,000 for his capture and $5,000 for information leading to it.

In the months after his Little Bohemia escape, Dillinger and a pal had lived for several weeks in a truck and moved from place to place on a moment's notice. But with his new face—though it looked quite a bit like the old one—he began to grow confident, even smug, about his ability to remain in plain view.

He took up with a new girlfriend, Polly Hamilton. He spent time at her apartment and ultimately moved in with her. They had company, sharing the space with Anna Sage, a forty-two-year-old who had been convicted for prostitution, and her grown son. Unknown to Dillinger, the United States was trying to send Sage back to her native Romania.

Dillinger told Hamilton he was a Chicago Board of Trade employee named Jimmy Lawrence, and together they enjoyed the summer. They took in Chicago Cubs games, visited the World's Fair, and went to movies. At night, they went dancing. He became a regular at the neighborhood ice-cream parlor and barbershop.

Though Sage figured out who he was from newspaper photos, he trusted both women to protect him.

In mid-July, Sage received a letter telling her that her appeals had run out and her deportation was near. She called an old police friend,

Anna Sage in July 1934

an East Chicago, Illinois, detective, and told him that Dillinger was dating Hamilton—neglecting to mention that all three were sharing an apartment. She was willing to work with police if they could help her. The detective put her in touch with the federal bureau's Chicago office.

On Saturday, July 21, Sage met Melvin Purvis, the man who had let Dillinger slip away several times before. She told him that she could help deliver Dillinger—if he could help her with her immigration issue. He said he would do what he could. (He also didn't ask many questions; if he had, he might have learned where Dillinger was living.)

Sage told him that Dillinger would probably take her and Hamilton to the movies on Sunday night. She would wear an orange skirt so they would know who she was.

From Washington, Hoover gave specific instructions: He wanted Dillinger taken alive, if at all possible.

On July 22, Sage let Hoover's agents know they would be going to either the Biograph or the Marbro Theater. The agents, working with East Chicago police (but not the Chicago police who had long tracked Dillinger) would stake out both of them.

A little after 8:30 p.m., Hamilton, Sage, and Dillinger, dressed in gray slacks, white shirt, eyeglasses, and a straw hat, walked up to the Biograph Theater, where Clark Gable was starring in *Manhattan Melodrama*. Under the lights, Sage's skirt looked bright red. Dillinger bought tickets and the three went inside to take seats in a packed house.

Outside, agents and East Chicago police took their spots to follow Dillinger as soon as he emerged. Purvis would give a signal: He would light his cigar as soon as he saw them.

At 10:40 p.m., Dillinger and the two women pushed through the front doors of the theater. Purvis lit his cigar, but only a few of the sixteen agents stationed nearby saw him. As the trio moved forward, three agents moved in behind Dillinger and pulled out their pistols. Sensing the danger, Dillinger reached into his pocket to get his gun. He stepped ahead of the women, looking as if he was going to make a break for a nearby alley.

None of the men called "Stop" or "Halt," or tried to make an arrest. Instead, all three agents fired, hitting him once in the side, grazing him twice, and hitting him in the back of the neck. Dillinger fell face forward into the alley.

In the mayhem, two bystanders were hit in the legs by flying bullets, though not seriously wounded. Within moments of the shooting, the curious began to crowd forward to see what had happened. A dozen agents tried to push them back.

The Biograph Theater after Dillinger was shot

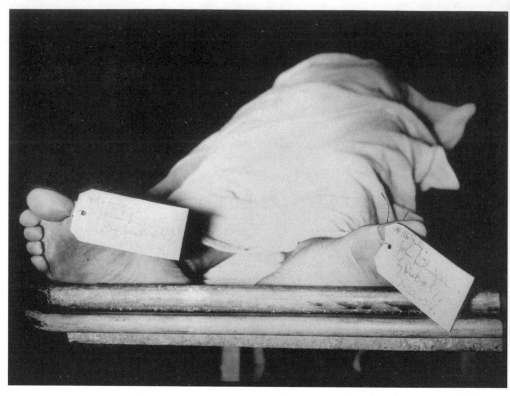

Toe tags mark the body of John Dillinger in the county morgue.

An ambulance picked up Dillinger. After a coroner declared him dead, he was taken to the county morgue. Hundreds of people began to gather to see the body.

As word spread that Dillinger had been shot, others gathered at the Biograph Theater. Men dipped handkerchiefs and women dipped their skirts into the blood on the sidewalk as souvenirs.

Hamilton and Sage went into hiding. Two days later, a boy found a Thompson submachine gun, a pistol, and a bulletproof vest in Lake Michigan. The Tommy gun was one Dillinger had stolen from an Indiana police department. Chicago police theorized that Sage had cleaned out the apartment and thrown Dillinger's things in the lake.

Before long, the press was reporting that a mysterious "woman in red" gave Dillinger up. Sage's gamble didn't pay off, however. She was sent back to Romania, where she died in 1947.

Pretty Boy Floyd was next.

In the aftermath of the train station murders in Kansas City, Floyd knew he was a hunted man. In September 1933, with his running buddy Adam Richetti, and a pair of sisters who were their girlfriends, he rented an apartment in Buffalo, New York, under an assumed name. For a year, the four lived in the tight quarters, playing cards, eating spaghetti, and enjoying Floyd's apple pies. Afraid to go out much, Floyd paced the floor every night and carefully tracked the news.

Though both Floyd and Richetti were in Kansas City at the time of the Union Station shooting, Floyd repeatedly denied any role in it. He even sent a letter to Kansas City police saying so.

Hoover's men were running out of leads. One by one, the bureau marked off crooks who also denied being at Union Station. In March 1934, it stumbled on what it believed to be firm evidence: A fingerprint of Richetti's was found on a beer bottle at the home of Verne Miller, the hired shooter who was almost certainly at the massacre. Miller had been mysteriously murdered in Detroit in 1933, likely by gang members. That left Floyd as the best-known living suspect in the killing of the federal agents.

After Dillinger was killed, Floyd became the new Public Enemy No. 1.

In October, an eager government informant told federal agents that Miller had been introduced to Floyd and Richetti and hired them. Knowing the hunt would intensify, Floyd, now thirty years old, and his

PUEBLO

887

friends decided to return to Oklahoma. His money was running low and he was tired of feeling as if he were serving time in prison again.

He made it only as far as Ohio. When his car slid off a road and crashed in a rural area, he and Richetti sent the women to find a repair shop while they stayed behind. A farmer, finding them suspicious, called police. In a shoot-out, Richetti was arrested. Floyd fired off a few shots with his Tommy gun, but it jammed; he escaped into the woods.

The feds were alerted. Melvin Purvis happened to be in Ohio. A day later, acting partly on a tip and partly out of luck, he and his men caught up with Floyd as he tried to get a ride out of town. Darting out of a car, Floyd refused to stop and surrender. He was shot twice running across an open field.

Confronted as he lay dying, he admitted he was Charles Floyd. But he refused to admit to any part in the Kansas City shooting.

In November, the feds got Baby Face Nelson, cornering him as he returned from a quick trip to Wisconsin. In a grisly roadside shoot-out in suburban Chicago, one agent sprayed fifty bullets from a Tommy gun at Nelson, hitting him several times in the stomach. Another fired ten times with a sawed-off shotgun, hitting Nelson in the legs. Angry and undeterred, Nelson managed to shoot both of them with his Thompson, killing one immediately. The other agent died the next day.

Hoover would tell reporters that he was "grieved beyond words" at the loss of two of his men.

Though bleeding profusely and badly injured, Nelson was able to climb into a car with his wife and accomplice, and leave the scene. His

Knowing he was wanted, Pretty Boy Floyd spent a year holed up in an apartment in Buffalo, New York.

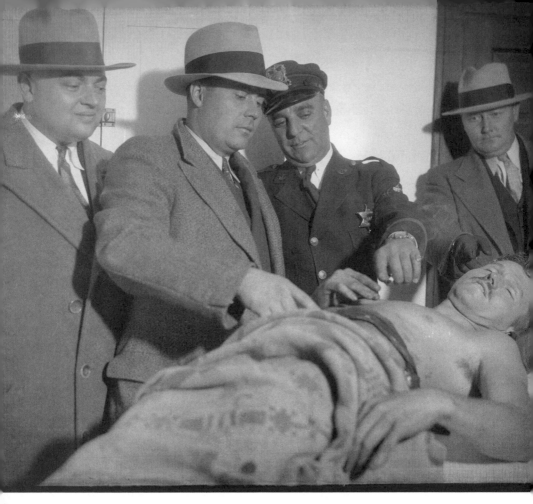

Police stand over the body of Baby Face Nelson after it was found in a ditch following a deadly shoot-out the day before.

dead body, with seventeen bullet wounds, was found wrapped in a blanket in a ditch the next day.

○ ○ ○ ○

Al Capone, the most violent and dangerous man of the 1920s, had the opportunity to defend himself in a trial before being sentenced to prison. Many of the most prominent 1930s-era bank robbers and gang members didn't have that option: They were shot dead on the streets.

A cartoon highlights the different kinds of justice meted out after the federal government won new police powers.

Though a few, such as George Kelly, were tried and convicted, at least a dozen others died during intense manhunts that reflected the shoot-to-kill mentality of a new and evolving federal police force. Generally, the press and the public applauded the violent endings and lauded the bravery of the federal men or local police.

Attorney General Homer Cummings called news of Dillinger's death "exceedingly gratifying as well as reassuring."

Hoover was quick to promote his agents' bravery and commitment in tracking the men down. "The only thing these gangsters fear is death," he said. "They don't mind jails, because they can get out of them or be released on parole—the biggest racket in the country. But they fear a man who meets them with his gun and can shoot quicker and straighter than they do."

He went on, "People said I gave orders not to bring Dillinger in alive. I did not. Dillinger tried to pull his gun." He added, embelishing the facts, "Only three shots were fired and every one hit him in the head."

The coroner made a death mask of Dillinger's face, and for years, Hoover displayed it just outside his office, along with the straw hat Dillinger wore that night, a photo from his pocket, and the eyeglasses he had on, with one lens rim shattered by a bullet. On display nearby were machine guns, revolvers, and other weapons once carried by criminals.

An FBI display of its Dillinger collection

Only a few critics questioned why the federal government needed to spend $500,000 tracking down a man who wasn't exactly hiding out. Or whether trigger fingers had to be so quick, noting that federal agents shot Dillinger—in the back, no less—although the only federal crime he had committed was taking a car across state lines.

Saying that Cummings told Hoover's men in May 1934 to "shoot to kill—then count ten," one writer noted that he "was violating not only the rights of the several states to enforce their own laws but the right of a suspected automobile thief not to be shot on sight."

Hoover was also criticized for taking way too much credit. After all, Dillinger was caught thanks to tips from the East Chicago police, and local officials first stumbled on Pretty Boy Floyd. Better cooperation between the bureau and local police might have avoided the embarrassment of Little Bohemia and other missed chances to stop the outlaws.

Still, as the bureau finally began to have some success, it got some help from an unexpected ally. In 1930, as the Depression was beginning, the movie industry had agreed to a code of behavior that was intended to enforce good morals and support the Ten Commandments. Courts portrayed in the movies would be fair, police would be portrayed as honest, and criminals weren't supposed to earn a viewer's sympathy. All of this was intended to make sure that movies didn't teach people to be criminals and that viewers—especially children and teenagers—didn't find crime attractive.

After adopting the code, the movie industry largely ignored it.

But almost parallel with the war on crime, Catholic and Protestant clergy, parent-teacher organizations, and women's groups were growing increasingly outspoken about the violence and sex in popular movies. Several states and cities already had censorship boards that reviewed movies and clipped out sections that they thought their communities shouldn't see. Religious and women's groups began calling for more censorship and even boycotts of movies nationwide.

In response, Hollywood agreed to begin enforcing the moral code in mid-1934, a decision that affected movie content well into the 1960s, when the current movie rating system was adopted. (*Manhattan Melodrama,* the movie Dillinger saw just before his demise, was one of the last to avoid a moral-code review.)

Suddenly, crimes committed in movies had to be punished and movie criminals couldn't be heroes—which played right into the growing publicity about Hoover's well-publicized "G-men." Instead of movies about public enemies or Capone or Dillinger, films began to glorify lawmen, especially federal agents.

In 1935, James Cagney carried a Tommy gun, this time playing a successful federal agent in *G Men*, a blockbuster movie that helped turn FBI men into pop culture icons. That movie spawned others.

At the same time, Hoover and publicity men he hired turned out books and magazine articles and encouraged cartoon strips touting the work of clever and brave federal agents. Before long, G-men replaced gangsters as the stars of the later 1930s. G-men toys, including play guns, badges, and cars, and even G-men pajamas, followed.

Now when little kids played with their colorful toy Tommy guns and pistols, they were truly on the side of law and order.

In *G Men*, James Cagney carried a Tommy gun as an FBI man, rather than as a criminal.

GM. 147

CHAPTER 15

THE END OF AN ERA

SOMETHING ELSE unexpected happened in the aftermath of the war on crime. The Thompson submachine gun just about disappeared from the streets. Only on rare occasions did police face machine-gun fire.

The National Firearms Act, no doubt, was a significant factor. The tax on purchasing the guns doubled the cost, making a new gun the equivalent of about $7,000 in today's dollars. In addition, being caught without registration was automatic legal trouble.

Federal Laboratories still handled sales of new Tommy guns, but domestic machine-gun sales dried up after the National Firearms Act was passed. For legitimate buyers—and for crooks as well—semiautomatic handguns, revolvers, and other weapons would do the job with fewer consequences.

In the first six months of the law, almost 16,000 firearms were registered and twenty-one dealers paid fees to continue reselling automatic weapons, bringing the government all of $4,000. Two years later, in 1936, just one person paid the $200 tax to buy or transfer a gun. Still, by 1937, more than 9,300 submachine guns, 11,520 machines guns and machine rifles, and more than 16,000 sawed-off shotguns and rifles had been registered with the federal government.

Firearm deaths nationwide from homicides, suicides, and accidents peaked around 1933, and then declined all the way through the World War II years. They didn't return to 1930s levels again until the mid-1960s.

The National Rifle Association breathed a sigh of relief at limiting regulations to machine guns and sawed-off shotguns—but warned its members to keep their guard up. It pointed out to its readers that just weeks after the new law was passed, a St. Louis federal agent killed Desse Masterson, a mother of four, in a raid while looking for a machine gun used in a murder. The Masterson family had just moved into the house three days before. When no one opened the door, the agent opened fire. Masterson's nine-year-old daughter was on the bed next to her when she was shot.

Fortunately, the NRA wrote in an editorial, "relatively few innocent citizens may be expected to be killed by federal agents looking for *machine guns*." But, it pointed out, agents looking for pistols and revolvers would have been a different matter.

As the NRA feared, Homer Cummings continued his efforts to include small weapons—and even rifles and shotguns—under federal gun laws. Under one proposal, he would expand the National Firearms Act to require their registration and assess a $1 tax for each weapon transferred. Calling gun registration even simpler than auto registration, he said, "No honest man can object to it. Show me the man who does not want his gun registered and I will show you a man who should not have a gun."

His pleas once again failed to win over Congress. However, in 1938, Congress passed the Federal Firearms Act, which required manufacturers, dealers, and importers of firearms who dealt in interstate or international commerce to obtain a federal license (for $1) and keep a record of sales. It also prohibited interstate shipment of firearms to convicted felons.

In 1939, in the case of *United States v. Miller*, the U.S. Supreme Court upheld the National Firearms Act, allowing the federal government to tax certain weapons and require their registration. The law would stand.

In the 1930s, the Thompson submachine gun finally began to get some respect from the U.S. military.

The U.S. Navy had adopted it in 1928 and used it successfully in Nicaragua. After testing the gun again in 1931, the U.S. Army noted that men who use it "had become very fond of this weapon and expressed a preference for it for use in battle." Still, it adopted the Tommy gun only for limited uses in 1932. Finally, in 1938, two decades after John Thompson conceived it, the army agreed to make it a standard-issue weapon.

By then, Auto-Ordnance had sold 10,300 guns, leaving more than 4,000 still in inventory. The Ryan family was still losing money on it every year.

Marcellus Thompson had tried for years to find ways to sell the company and benefit from his family's minority interest, but each effort failed. Finally, in 1939, he was introduced to Russell Maguire, an entrepreneur who had found a niche investing in troubled businesses throughout the Depression. Though the company seemed to have

Russell Maguire, sensing an opportunity, bought control of Auto-Ordnance just as the Second World War was breaking out in Europe.

potential, that wasn't obvious from appearances. Its manufacturing equipment was old and dusty, it had few new orders, and new guns hadn't been made in years. Still, Maguire agreed with Marcellus Thompson that a possible war could be an unseen opportunity. Writing about the planned sale, *Time* magazine called the Tommy gun "the deadliest weapon, pound for pound, ever devised by man."

To acquire the company, the two had to raise enough money to buy out the Ryan family. Ultimately, the Ryan family agreed to sell at a deep discount, but with a huge requirement: If Thompson didn't make the first payment by July 21, 1939, his family would lose its minority interest forever. Then the Ryans could do what they wanted with the company.

Lining up a bank loan took longer than expected, bringing Marcellus Thompson right up to the deadline. On July 21, an exhausted Thompson sat down to work through the papers that had to be read and signed. Midmorning, he collapsed and was rushed to the hospital. At fifty-six years old, he had suffered a debilitating stroke.

With Marcellus deathly ill, Maguire suddenly demanded more compensation. Negotiations went down to the wire—until one of Maguire's men returned from the hospital claiming to have Marcellus's signature of approval. The sale closed with just fifteen minutes to spare.

Within months, orders began rolling in to Auto-Ordnance, first from the French, then the British, and the Russians. The United States wasn't far behind. In the course of World War II, the Thompson submachine gun would finally be sold for its intended purpose: helping Americans win on the battlefield.

For John and Marcellus Thompson, it should have been redemption on a grand scale. But neither would live to see their baby make its mark in war.

Marcellus never recovered from his stroke. He died three months later, on October 17, 1939, leaving behind his second wife, Evelyn, three daughters, and his father.

Widowed in 1930, John Thompson had moved in with his son in his retirement. He spent his later years in a wheelchair or in bed, with dimming eyesight and limited mobility. Even so, he remained alert and

John Thompson, around 1930

upbeat and continued to write his old Auto-Ordnance colleagues about his "T.S.M.G." Always the loyal military man, he was pleased to pass along the news to Theodore Eickhoff in 1938 that "the T.S.M.G. has *at last* been adopted by the War Dept."

In his later years, he also grew reflective, sharing pangs of conscience about what he had created. In a last letter to Eickhoff just before Marcellus died, Thompson wrote, "I often think of you and our happy old days at Chester and Washington, D.C."

But his life and perspective had changed. "I have given *my valedictory* to arms, as I want to pay more attention now to saving human life than destroying it. May the deadly T.S.M.G. always 'speak' for God and Country. It has worried me that the gun has been so *stolen* by evil men & used for purposes outside our motto, 'On the side of law & order.'"

He told his friend he had been sick and confined to bed, but concluded, "I am happy & keep a peaceful mind."

John T. Thompson died on June 21, 1940, at the age of seventy-nine, leaving behind a weapon with a history far greater and more complex than he ever intended.

LEGACY

THE THOMPSON SUBMACHINE GUN may have seen its glory days in the 1920s and 1930s, but it truly fulfilled John Thompson's vision during World War II.

As the only such gun that was ready and well tested, the Tommy gun was suddenly in great demand, despite its advancing age and relatively high price. It "gained considerable popularity with the troops in the field because of its fire power," according to an army history.

As the military and Auto-Ordnance revved up to produce new guns, they found ways to cut costs with each new model and to make the guns even lighter. While soldiers may have felt they were blazing away with gangster guns, the weapons they used were different: The front pistol grip disappeared, the Blish lock was dumped as unnecessary, and the weight was reduced. Soldiers experimented with a forty-cartridge magazine by putting two twenty-bullet magazines together with

electrician's tape, but officials settled on a new thirty-cartridge rectangular magazine.

With such efficiencies, the price for a Thompson submachine gun fell from $70 in 1942 to $45, with accessories and spare parts, in 1944.

Altogether, Auto-Ordnance made about 1.75 million new Thompson guns. In the last two years of the war, however, the Tommy gun was largely replaced by a lighter and cheaper submachine gun, the M3, nicknamed the "grease gun" because it resembled a mechanic's tool.

When the war was over, so was the effective life of the Thompson submachine gun. As the old guns changed hands, they showed up around the world, including in Latin America and Vietnam, and again in Ireland. But meaningful orders for new guns disappeared, this time for good.

The remnants of Auto-Ordnance were sold several times. Today, you will still find a version of Auto-Ordnance on the Internet, primarily for Tommy gun enthusiasts. Owned by Kahr Firearms Group, the company sells a display-model Tommy gun, a semiautomatic Thompson replica, and accessories—including well-padded violin cases.

Once his G-men reached cult-hero status, Hoover went on to run the agency with an iron fist until he died in 1972 at age seventy-seven, serving a total of forty-eight years as director.

Over those years, Hoover built the FBI into an efficient and reputable national investigative agency that won respect for its ability to combat crime and support local law enforcement.

British Prime Minister Winston Churchill tries out a Tommy gun during a visit with troops in 1940.

But continuing a practice he started early in his career, Hoover also used his power to pump up his own stature and to spy on hundreds of thousands of Americans. The FBI under Hoover kept detailed and gossipy files on suspected communists, politicians, and political activists, including civil rights leaders such as Dr. Martin Luther King, Jr., which were sometimes used to smear their reputations. Though he fought the Depression-era outlaws, Hoover refused to acknowledge or investigate the growth of the Mafia for decades.

In response to revelations about how he ran the bureau, FBI directors are now limited to ten-year terms.

Though long gone, the roar of the Thompson gun still echoes today in our nation's approach toward guns and in the divisive debate over gun rights and gun laws.

In the more than eighty years since Homer Cummings used Dillinger's rampage to secure the National Firearms Act, only a handful of additional federal gun laws have been adopted.

In the 1960s, amid an increase in gun violence and the assassinations of President John F. Kennedy, his brother Robert Kennedy, and Dr. King, Congress passed the first new gun laws since the 1930s. Worried about more gun regulation, new leaders took over at the National Rifle Association in the mid-1970s and adopted an aggressive approach to opposing new laws, saying that guns were about self-defense, and their ownership was protected under the Second Amendment. Gun laws weren't about community safety, but about taking away constitutional rights from gun owners.

"We must declare that there are no shades of gray in American freedom," Wayne LaPierre, NRA executive vice president, said in 2002, summarizing the group's position. "You're with us or against us." With its new stance, the NRA became one of the most influential voices in American politics, reshaping the gun debate.

In most states today, you can still easily buy guns at a local store, including those resembling military weapons. That continues to surprise some people. But there are restrictions: Those convicted of a felony or of domestic violence, drug users, and the mentally ill are prohibited from buying a gun. People who buy handguns from federally licensed dealers, such as a typical retail store, must be at least twenty-one years old and pass a background check. Licensed dealers must keep track of sales so that guns used in crimes can be traced.

However, under federal law, an eighteen-year-old can buy a handgun from a private dealer, such as those who sell at gun shows, and the federal government doesn't require background checks for guns purchased from those unlicensed sellers. Those dealers account for an estimated two in five sales.

Since 1986, manufacturing new automatic weapons like the Tommy gun for civilian use in the United States has been illegal. (Qualified buyers can still purchase an automatic weapon made before 1986 if they complete the paperwork and pay the tax, which remains $200.)

As in the 1920s and 1930s, the majority of gun deaths and injuries today result from relatively inexpensive handguns. But the descendants of the Tommy gun—powerful, fast-firing semiautomatic weapons created for military use—continue to grab the headlines and generate controversy.

In 1994, following a series of mass shootings that involved military-style weapons, Congress approved a ten-year ban on so-called assault weapons—semiautomatics with some military-weapon features, such as certain AK-47s and AR-15s. The law outlawed nineteen specific weapons and magazines of more than ten rounds, but didn't affect the 1.5 million such weapons already legally owned.

When the law expired in 2004, Congress didn't renew it.

Gun groups argued then and argue today that the lines between these firearms and others are much blurrier than they were in the 1930s. The National Shooting Sports Foundation says that such semiautomatic weapons are really standard firearms, used in marksmanship competitions and for hunting. They are "functionally no different" than other firearms, it says.

In June 2008, the U.S. Supreme Court addressed the Second Amendment for the first time in the nearly seventy years since it had upheld the National Firearms Act. This time, it tackled the contemporary question of whether the twenty-seven-word amendment, with its preface about "a well regulated militia," gives an individual the right to own guns for personal use.

The case, *District of Columbia v. Heller*, dealt with a tough Washington, D.C., law that banned handguns and required legally owned guns to be unloaded and disassembled, or locked up when they were stored in one's home. Dick Heller, a security guard, challenged the law, arguing he had a right to have a workable gun in his home.

In a five-to-four decision, the Supreme Court agreed, saying the amendment protects an individual's right to own a weapon and use it for legal purposes, such as self-defense in one's home. It was a landmark ruling. Despite the long-running debate about individual rights, all Second Amendment issues up until then had been decided through the lens of a militia and militia participation.

In its decision, the court made clear that individual rights aren't unlimited and that the Constitution leaves room for gun restrictions. For instance, the court said in its opinion, its decision shouldn't "cast doubt on longstanding prohibitions on the possession of firearms by felons and the mentally ill, or laws forbidding the carrying of firearms in sensitive places such as schools and government buildings, or laws imposing conditions and qualifications on the commercial sale of arms." It also recognized the "historical tradition of prohibiting the carrying of 'dangerous and unusual weapons,'" such as the sawed-off shotguns and submachine guns restricted by the National Firearms Act.

In refusing to allow an outright ban on handguns, the court underscored that guns and gun ownership in America are not all-or-nothing issues. Owning a gun for self-defense still comes with limits. The community has rights, too, including the right to be safe. The historian Saul Cornell notes, "The Second Amendment belongs to all Americans."

In 2012, two frightening and deeply disturbing mass shootings renewed calls for another look at background checks, gun registration, and assault weapons. In July, a heavily armed twenty-four-year-old graduate student opened fire in a theater in Aurora, Colorado, during a midnight showing of a new Batman movie, killing twelve people and

A makeshift memorial on the highway near Newtown, Connecticut, honors the memory of the children, teachers, and staff killed in a mass shooting at Sandy Hook Elementary School.

injuring seventy more. In December, a twenty-year-old man killed his mother and headed to Sandy Hook Elementary School in Newtown, Connecticut, with an arsenal of weapons. There he murdered twenty small schoolchildren and six adults before killing himself.

Despite pleas from parents, President Barack Obama, and others in the aftermath, Congress was unable to agree on any changes to the existing gun laws.

Still, the debate thunders on. As they have throughout American history, guns still give power and voice to people who might not otherwise have them. And with roughly 300 million guns in America—about one gun for every resident—real concerns remain about gun violence in our communities.

Though gun-murder rates have declined since their peak in the early 1990s, about 32,000 Americans still die from gunshots each year—about 11,000 from murder and an additional 20,000 from suicide. That's just a couple of thousand fewer than die in car accidents.

Young people are especially affected. Older teens and young adults under twenty-five years old are far more likely to die from a gunshot than any other age group. The Children's Defense Fund, a child-advocacy group, says that black children and teens are twice as likely to be killed by a gun than to die in a car accident.

As in the 1920s and 1930s, the causes of gun violence are complex, deeply intertwined with some of America's greatest social, economic, and political challenges. Gangs are one major problem, but so are dangerous urban neighborhoods, exposure to crime and violence, the illegal drug trade, lax gun safety, availability of guns, and mental-health issues.

In early 2013, after a spate of teen murders in Chicago, President Obama expressed his concern in a speech to a high school there. Gang gunfire had just killed an innocent fifteen-year-old girl, an honor student who had marched in his second inaugural parade. Such a murder, he said, is "not unique to Chicago. It's not unique to this country. Too many of our children are being taken away from us."

In fact, he said, sixty-five teens were murdered with firearms in Chicago in 2012. "That's the equivalent of a Newtown every four months," he added.

Though teens aren't legally allowed to buy guns, a national survey found that 44 percent believed they could get one. How? Much the way Dillinger and Capone did, either by stealing them or through middle-men who sell them on the streets.

Agreed-on solutions have proven difficult to come by, as has finding the right balance between individual freedom and community safety.

Do we need fewer guns or more of them? New technology, such as smart guns that work only for a gun's owner? More police or more neighborhood involvement?

This is the challenge that persists: How to effectively address the consequences of powerful weapons in the wrong hands. That's the complex legacy of the Tommy gun that still reverberates today.

BIBLIOGRAPHY

Any serious look at the history of the Thompson submachine gun must begin with William J. Helmer's book, *The Gun That Made the Twenties Roar*. What began as a master's thesis turned into an exquisitely researched book, published in 1969, that included interviews and correspondence with some of the gun's early developers. Though the book has long been out of print, virtually everything written about the Tommy gun since then draws on this work.

In a different way, Tracie Hill's massive volume, *The Ultimate Thompson Book,* offers detailed information for enthusiasts and collectors, including many historical documents and photographs. It's an excellent resource for those who want to know more about the gun itself. More information is also available from the American Thompson Association, nfatoys.com/tsmg/TheAmericanThompsonAssociation.

There are many sources on John Dillinger and the Depression-era outlaws, but the best place to start is with Bryan Burrough's *Public Enemies: America's Greatest Crime Wave and the Birth of the FBI, 1933–34.*

My research took me to the National Archives at College Park, Maryland, for details on military testing of the weapons, the investigation into the Irish gun-running scandal, and J. Edgar Hoover's scrapbooks and cartoons; the Library of Congress; The National Firearms Museum Library in Fairfax, Virginia; and the Hatton W. Sumners Papers at the Dallas Historical Society.

For more understanding about nineteenth- and twentieth-century guns, I interviewed William F. Atwater, director emeritus of the U.S. Army Ordnance Museum, and Doug Wicklund, senior curator at the National Firearms Museum.

As is often the case with research, dates, ages, and other details at times differed in different publications. Whenever possible, I tried to find a primary source to settle the disparity.

Also, for clarity, I have used a single name, the Bureau of Investigation, for the predecessor to the Federal Bureau of Investigation. During the time period covered, it was known as the Bureau of Investigation and the Division of Investigation. It didn't become the FBI until 1935.

I have listed key resources below and in the notes, but they are only some of the sources I consulted. If you have any questions about sources or facts, please contact me through my website, www.karenblumenthal.com.

Thompson Submachine Guns and Other Guns

Armstrong, David A. *Bullets and Bureaucrats: The Machine Gun and the United States Army, 1861–1916*. Westport, CT: Greenwood Press, 1982.

Barrett, Paul M. *Glock: The Rise of America's Gun*. New York: Broadway Paperbacks, 2013.

Browning, John and Curt Gentry. *John M. Browning: American Gunmaker*. Garden City, NY: Doubleday & Company, Inc., 1964.

Calabi, Silvio, Steve Helsley, and Roger Sanger. *The Gun Book for Boys*. Rockport, ME: Shooting Sportsman Books, 2012.

Chinn, George M. *The Machine Gun: History, Evolution, and Development of Manual, Automatic, and Airborne Repeating Weapons, Vol. 1*. Washington, DC: U.S. Government Printing Office, 1951.

Chivers, C. J. *The Gun*. New York: Simon & Schuster, 2010.

Eickhoff, Theodore H. "The Development of the Thompson Submachine Gun." Accessed at www.mikesmachineguns.com and in Tracie L. Hill, *The Ultimate Thompson Book,* pp. 9–39.

Ellis, John. *The Social History of the Machine Gun*. New York: Pantheon Books, 1975.

Helmer, William J. *The Gun That Made the Twenties Roar*. New York: The Macmillan Company, 1969.

Hill, Tracie L. *The Ultimate Thompson Book*. Ontario, Canada: Collector Grade Publications Incorporated, 2009.

Keller, Julia. *Mr. Gatling's Terrible Marvel: The Gun That Changed Everything and the Misunderstood Genius Who Invented It*. New York: Viking, 2008.

Kyle, Chris, with William Doyle. *American Gun: A History of the U.S. in Ten Firearms.* New York: William Morrow, 2013.

La Garde, Col. Louis A. *Gunshot Injuries: How They Are Inflicted, Their Complications and Treatment.* New York: William Wood and Company, 1916.

The National Cyclopaedia of American Biography. Ann Arbor, MI: University Microfilms, 1967.

Parker, John H. *The Gatlings at Santiago.* Kansas City, MO: Press of the Hudson-Kimberly Publishing Co., 1898.

Thompson, J. T. "Modern Weapons of War: A paper read before the Contemporary Club, Davenport, Iowa." Davenport, IA: The Contemporary Club, Richard Borcherdt, Printer, 1905.

Yenne, Bill. *Tommy Gun: How General Thompson's Submachine Gun Wrote History.* New York: St. Martin's Press, 2009.

Gangsters and Crime

Eig, Jonathan. *Get Capone: The Secret Plot That Captured America's Most Wanted Gangster.* New York: Simon & Schuster, 2010.

Giradin, G. Russell and William J. Helmer. *Dillinger: The Untold Story,* expanded edition. Bloomington, IN: Indiana University Press, 2005.

Hamilton, Stanley. *Machine Gun Kelly's Last Stand.* Lawrence, KS: University Press of Kansas, 2003.

Helmer, William J. and Rick Mattix. *The Complete Public Enemy Almanac: New Facts and Features on the People, Places, and Events of the Gangster and Outlaw Era: 1920–1940.* Nashville, TN: Cumberland House, 2007.

Illinois Association for Criminal Justice, "Illinois Crime Survey, 1929." https://homicide.northwestern.edu/pubs/icc/

Keefe, Rose. *Guns and Roses: The Untold Story of Dean O'Banion, Chicago's Big Shot Before Al Capone.* Nashville, TN: Cumberland House, 2002.

Kobler, John. *Capone: The Life and World of Al Capone.* Cambridge, MA: Da Capo Press, 2003.

Pasley, Fred D. *Al Capone: The Biography of a Self-Made Man*. Salem, NH: Ayer Company Publishers, Inc., 1971.

Schoenberg, Robert J. *Mr. Capone: The Real—and Complete—Story of Al Capone*. New York: Quill William Morrow, 1992.

Toland, John. *The Dillinger Days*. New York: Da Capo Press, 1995.

Wallis, Michael. *Pretty Boy: The Life and Times of Charles Arthur Floyd*. New York: St. Martin's Press, 1992.

The NRA

Rodengen, Jeffrey L. *NRA: An America Legend*. Fort Lauderdale, FL: Write Stuff Enterprises, 2002.

Trefethen, James B., compiler. *Americans and Their Guns: The National Rifle Association Story through Nearly a Century of Service to the Nation*. Edited by James E. Serven. Harrisburg, PA: Stackpole Books, 1967.

J. Edgar Hoover, the FBI, and 1930s crime

Aronson, Marc. *Master of Deceit: J. Edgar Hoover and America in the Age of Lies*. Somerville, MA: Candlewick Press, 2012.

Burrough, Bryan. *Public Enemies: America's Greatest Crime Wave and the Birth of the FBI, 1933–34*. New York: Penguin Books, 2004.

Denenberg, Barry. *The True Story of J. Edgar Hoover and the FBI*. New York: Scholastic Inc., 1993.

Gentry, Curt. *J. Edgar Hoover: The Man and the Secrets*. New York: W.W. Norton & Co., 1991.

Hoover, J. Edgar. *Persons in Hiding*. London: J.M. Dent & Sons Ltd., 1938.

Powers, Richard Grid. *Secrecy and Power: The Life of J. Edgar Hoover*. New York: The Free Press, 1987.

Theoharis, Athan G. and John Stuart Cox. *The Boss: J. Edgar Hoover and the Great American Inquisition*. Philadelphia: Temple University Press, 1988.

Unger, Robert. *The Union Station Massacre: The Original Sin of J. Edgar Hoover's FBI.* Kansas City, MO: Andrews McMeel Publishing, 1997.

Whitehead, Don. *The FBI Story: A Report to the People.* New York: Random House, 1956.

Gun Laws and Gun History

Bartoletti, Susan Campbell. *They Called Themselves the K.K.K.: The Birth of an American Terrorist Group.* Boston: Houghton Mifflin Harcourt, 2010.

Brown, Donald Curtis. *The Great Gun-Toting Controversy, 1865–1910: The Old West Gun Culture and Public Shootings.* Dissertation for Tulane University, 1983. Photocopy. Ann Arbor, MI: University Microfilms International, 1989.

Cook, Philip J. and Kristin A. Goss. *The Gun Debate: What Everyone Needs to Know.* Oxford: Oxford University Press, 2014.

Cornell, Saul. *A Well Regulated Militia: The Founding Fathers and the Origins of Gun Control in America.* New York: Oxford University Press, 2006.

DeConde, Alexander. *Gun Violence in America: The Struggle for Control.* Boston: Northeastern University Press, 2001.

Halbrook, Stephen P. *That Every Man Be Armed: The Evolution of a Constitutional Right.* Albuquerque, NM: University of New Mexico Press, 1984.

Hearings before a Subcommittee of the Committee on Commerce, United States Senate, 73rd Congress, Second Session, on S. 885, S. 2258, and S. 3680, May 28 and 29, 1934.

Hearings before the Committee on Ways and Means, United States House of Representatives, 73rd Congress, Second Session, on H.R. 9066, April 15, 16 and May 14, 15, and 16, 1934.

Kennett, Lee and James LaVerne Anderson. *The Gun in America: The Origins of a National Dilemma.* Westport, CT: Greenwood Press, 1975.

Leff, Carol Skalnik and Mark H. Leff. "The Politics of Ineffectiveness: Federal Firearms Legislation, 1919–1938," *Annals of the American Academy of Political and Social Science,* May 1981.

Spitzer, Robert J. *The Politics of Gun Control.* Chatham, NJ: Chatham House Publishers, Inc., 1995.

———. *The Right to Bear Arms: Rights and Liberties under the Law.* Santa Barbara, CA: ABC-CLIO, Inc., 2001.

Swisher, Carl Brent, editor. *Selected Papers of Homer Cummings.* New York: Charles Scribner's Sons, 1939.

"Violations of Free Speech and Rights of Labor," Hearings before a Subcommittee of the Committee on Education and Labor, United States Senate, 75th Congress, First Session, S. Res. 266, Part 7; Second Session, Part 15-D; and 76th Congress, First Session, 1939, Report No. 6, Part 1 and Part 3.

Winkler, Adam. *Gun Fight: The Battle over the Right to Bear Arms in America.* New York: W.W. Norton & Company, 2011.

1920s and 1930s

Barry, Tom. *Guerilla Days in Ireland: A Firsthand Account of the Black and Tan War (1919–1921).* New York: The Devin-Adair Company, 1956.

Blumenthal, Karen. *Bootleg: Murder, Moonshine, and the Lawless Years of Prohibition.* New York: Roaring Brook Press, 2011.

———. *Six Days in October: The Stock Market Crash of 1929.* New York: Atheneum, 2002.

Bolden, Tonya. *FDR's Alphabet Soup: New Deal America, 1932–1939.* New York: Alfred A. Knopf, 2010.

Gansberg, Alan L. *Little Caesar: A Biography of Edward G. Robinson.* Lanham, MD: The Scarecrow Press, Inc., 2004.

Miller, Frank. *Censored Hollywood: Sex, Sin, & Violence on Screen.* Atlanta: Turner Publishing, Inc. 1994.

Movies

The Doorway to Hell. Directed by Archie Mayo. 1930. Burbank, CA: MGM Warner Archive Collection, 2012. Downloaded via Amazon Instant Video.

G Men. Directed by William Keighley. 1935. Burbank, CA: Warner Home Video, 2006. DVD.

Little Caesar. Directed by Mervyn LeRoy. 1930. Burbank, CA: Warner Home Video, 2005. DVD.

The Public Enemy. Directed by William A. Wellman. Burbank, CA: Warner Home Video, 2005. DVD.

Scarface. Directed by Howard Hawks. 1932. Universal City, CA: Universal Studios Home Entertainment, 2007. DVD.

Publications

American Rifleman, Arms and the Man, Army and Navy Journal, Chicago Daily News (1920s), *Chicago Tribune, Collier's, Los Angeles Times, Literary Digest, New York Times, Time* and *Washington Post*

Websites

http://www.bureauofmilitaryhistory.ie/bmhscarch/browse.jsp. The Bureau of Military History Collection, 1913–1921, in Ireland includes interviews with witnesses of the Irish rebellion.

www.fbi.gov. The Federal Bureau of Investigation includes many articles on Hoover, FBI history, and gangsters of the 1920s and 1930s, all from the FBI's perspective.

http://www.nssf.org/newsroom/writers/guide/index.cfm. The National Shooting Sports Foundation has a helpful glossary, *The Writers Guide to Firearms and Ammunition*, created from a gun advocate's perspective.

http://blogs.archives.gov/unwritten-record/2014/01/09/gangsters-g-men and-archivists/. The National Archives blog includes a video made of the Machine Gun Kelly–Urschel kidnapping and trial.

NOTES, QUOTES, AND OTHER DETAILS

Prologue: Locked and Loaded

John Enz: "Mountain Area Patrolled," *New York Times*, Oct. 16, 1926; Owen P. White, "Machine Guns for Sale," *Collier's*, Dec. 4, 1926, p. 13; "Mail Bandits Kill One and Shoot Three in Theft of $150,000 Cash at Elizabeth," *Newark Evening News,* Oct. 14, 1926, p. 1; "Bandits with Machine Gun Kill Man, Shoot Two," *New York Times*, Oct. 15, 1926; "2 Slain, 3 Wounded with Machine Gun in Chicago Street," *Washington Post*, Oct. 12, 1926; "Mail Bandits' Den in Hills Surrounded by State Cops; Coolidge's Cabinet May Act to Avert Federal Robberies," *Newark Star-Eagle*, Oct. 15, 1926; William J. Helmer, *The Gun That Made the Twenties Roar*, p. 85.

Quotes: "Most dangerous small arm": "Machine Gun's History Is Clue to Murders," *Newark Star-Eagle*, Oct. 15, 1926, p. 1.

"America's criminals": Edward H. Smith, "Machine Guns and Gas Are Easy to Purchase," *New York Times*, Nov. 21, 1926.

"What can we": Helmer, p. 85.

Chapter 1: Conception

The gun that shook Elizabeth: Auto-Ordnance Corporation, "Handbook of the Thompson Submachine Gun, Model of 1921," p. 57 (different models and prototypes of the Thompson submachine gun were made, but these are the dimensions of the most common model, the one that Colt manufactured in 1921).

Just after the Civil War: Julia Keller, *Mr. Gatling's Terrible Marvel*, pp. 7, 25, 27, 40, 152–154, 160–164, 166–168; David A. Armstrong, *Bullets and Bureaucrats,* pp. 98–99; John Ellis, *The Social History of the Machine Gun*, pp. 15–17, 50, 70; C. J. Chivers, *The Gun*, pp. 8, 88; George M. Chinn, *The Machine Gun,* pp. 48–58.

(The Gatling gun did make one rather horrifying appearance during the Civil War: In 1863, those who couldn't pay $300 to buy their way out of military service began to riot in New York City. At one point, an angry mob headed to the *New York Times* building. There, the feisty editor, Henry Jarvis Raymond, had stationed three Gatling guns in the windows; other staffers were armed with rifles. When the rioters saw the weapons, they retreated.)

Quotes: "It occurred to me": Keller, p. 7.

"the most effective implement": Keller, p. 40.

The Gatling gun wasn't formally tested: "Crucible of Empire: The Spanish-American War," http://www.pbs.org/crucible/frames/_timeline.html; John H. Parker, *The Gatlings at Santiago*, pp. 9–12, 22–50, 128–138; "An Able Officer Promoted," *Arms and the Man*, Oct. 30, 1913, p. 88; Armstrong, pp. 96–105; Helmer, pp. 3–4; Keller, pp. 204–206; Theodore Roosevelt, "Preface," in Parker, unpaged; "Gen. Thompson, 79, Arms Expert, Dies," *New York Times,* June 22, 1940.

Quotes: "were seen to melt": Parker, p. 136.

"Our artillery": Theodore Roosevelt, preface to Parker, unpaged.

Thompson's next assignment: Helmer, pp. 5–6; Interview with William F. Atwater, director emeritus, U.S. Army Ordnance Museum, May 14, 2014; Interview with Doug Wicklund, senior curator, National Firearms Museum, May 19, 2014. Col. Louis A. La Garde, *Gunshot Injuries,* pp. 64–78; Chivers, pp. 229–233 (Chivers notes that the data sample was small and later tests showed that bullet wounding was more complex, but the tests still were influential); Theodore H. Eickhoff, "The Development of the Thompson Submachine Gun," p. 2; "Thompson, John Taliaferro," *The National Cyclopaedia of American Biography,* pp. 298–299; Lee Kennett and James LaVerne Anderson, *The Gun in America,* pp. 138–141; James B. Trefethen, compiler, and James E. Serven, editor, *Americans and Their Guns,* pp. 34–35, 130; "For National Defense: Measure to Promote Target Practice Will Be Urged in Congress," *Baltimore Sun,* Jan 2, 1914.

Quotes: "stopping power and shock": La Garde, p. 69.

"The animals invariably": La Garde, p. 74.

"about a dozen": Eickhoff, p. 2.

By 1907, Thompson: J. T. Thompson, "Modern Weapons of War," pp. 72–79, 97; Chinn, p. 29; "An Able Officer Promoted," *Arms and the Man*, Oct. 30, 1913, p. 88; "Machine Guns," *American Mercury*, April 1928, pp. 452–456; "Colonel Thompson Retires," *Arms and the Man,* Nov. 12, 1914, p. 128; Helmer, pp. 9–10.

Quotes: "extreme humanitarians": Thompson, p. 72.

"an officer of exceptional ability": *Arms and the Man*, Oct. 30, 1913, p. 88.

"weapons of emergency" and "fire alone": *American Mercury*, April 1928, p. 454.

Chapter 2: Trench Broom

John Taliaferro Thompson had never actually designed a gun: Helmer, pp. 2–3, 20–25; "James Thompson," *The National Cyclopaedia of American Biography,* p. 297; A. R. Stanley, "Uncle Sam's Premier Gunman—Col. John T. Thompson," *Detroit Free Press,* July 28, 1918.

Quotes: "unusual and great," "particularly elated" and "Why you dumb bell": Eickhoff, pp. 5–6.

Around the world: Maj. Julian S. Hatcher, "Machine Guns," *American Rifleman,* June 1932, pp. 10–11; Chinn, pp. 173–177, 240–241; John Browning and Curt Gentry, *John M. Browning: American Gunmaker,* pp. 240–242; Interviews with William F. Atwater and Doug Wicklund; Eickhoff, pp. 7–12; Helmer, pp. 10–14, 22–25; Tracie L. Hill, *The Ultimate Thompson Book*, pp. 30–34.

Quotes: "No more crudely designed": Chinn, p. 240.

"Some near tragedies": Hatcher, p. 11.

"need a small machine gun": Hill, p. 34.

"a one-man, hand-held machine gun": Helmer, p. 25.

Chapter 3: The Annihilator

Within days of Thompson's request: Hill, pp. 18–19, 29, 35–37; Helmer, pp. 14, 16–19, 27–29; Eickhoff, pp. 9–10; V. B. Gray, "Death Rattles in These Guns," *Plain*

Dealer (Cleveland, OH), Oct. 24, 1920; "Social Notes," *New York Times,* Aug. 12, 1914; "In Mist from Sea, Miss Harvey Weds," *New York Times,* Aug. 13, 1914; "Mark Twain's Exclusive Publisher Tells What the Humorist Is Paid," *Washington Post,* March 3, 1907; "Col. George Harvey Dies in Dublin, N.H., *New York Times,* Aug. 21, 1926; "Ryan, the 'Most Noiseless' Man of American Finance," *New York Times*, May 19, 1907; "Thomas F. Ryan, the Sphinx of Wall Street," *New York Times*, June 18, 1905; "America's 30 Richest Own $3,680,000,000," *Forbes,* March 2, 1918.

Quotes: "I know all about you": Hill, pp. 18–19.

"jumbled bits of lead": *Plain Dealer* (Cleveland, OH), Oct. 24, 1920.

"I am afraid": *New York Times*, June 18, 1905.

"the most adroit": *New York Times*, May 19, 1907.

While Eickhoff and Payne: A. R. Stanley, "Uncle Sam's Premier Gunman—Col. John T. Thompson," *Detroit Free Press*, July 28, 1918; *The National Cyclopaedia of American Biography*, p. 299; Helmer, pp. 21, 29–34; "Chamberlain Repeats His Charges, Insists War Department Has Failed," *New York Times*, Jan. 25, 1918; "Four Get Honor Medals," *Washington Post,* March 4, 1919; Eickhoff, pp. 12–13; Hill, p. 39.

Quotes: "while the house was burning": *New York Times*, Jan. 25, 1918.

"America's premier gunman" and "My principle has been": *Detroit Free Press*, July 28, 1918.

"If you did something": Helmer, p. 21.

"other people's money": Helmer, p. 31.

"It looks like": Helmer, p. 32.

Chapter 4: Ready . . . Aim

Even though the war was over: Helmer, pp. 34–47; V. B. Gray, *Plain Dealer* (Cleveland, OH), Oct. 24, 1920; "Thompson Sub-Machine Gun," *Army and Navy Journal*, Oct. 2, 1920, p. 120; Eickhoff, pp. 13–14.

Quotes: "The raising of 100": *Army and Navy Journal*, Oct. 2, 1920, p. 120.

"the time was ripe": Eickhoff, p. 13.

"machine pistol" and "autogun": Helmer, p. 35.

"I'm no military man": Eickhoff, p. 14.

In 1920, the Thompsons: "The New Submachine Gun," *Army and Navy Journal*, Jan. 1, 1921, p. 519; Philip B. Sharpe, "The Thompson Sub-Machine Gun," *Journal of Criminal Law and Criminology*, March–April 1933, pp. 1098–1099, 1105; Helmer, pp. 48–51, 72; "Gotham Police to Use Machine Gun Pistol," *Philadelphia Inquirer*, Sept. 11, 1920; "Might Help in Kansas City," *Kansas City Star*, Sept. 19, 1920; "Weapon Aims at Crime, *Oregonian*, Jan. 23, 1921; "Police to Have a Machine Gun," *Los Angeles Times*, May 16, 1921; Hill, pp. 96–99; Auto-Ordnance Corporation, "Handbook of the Thompson Submachine Gun, Model of 1921," p. 57, Eickhoff, pp. 14–15; Capt. E. C. Crossman, "A Pocket Machine Gun," *Scientific American*, Oct. 16, 1920, pp. 405, 413–414.

Quotes: "a sheet of flame": Sharpe, p. 1098.

"one long roar": Sharpe, p. 1105.

"With it, it is claimed": *Kansas City Star*, Sept. 19, 1920.

"is guaranteed to put lead": *Oregonian*, Jan. 23, 1921.

"are going to have": *Los Angeles Times*, May 16, 1921.

"If it's worth a million": Helmer, p. 50.

"pocket machine gun": *Scientific American*, Oct. 16, 1920.

When the first guns: "Test of Thompson Machine Gun," *Army and Navy Journal*, April 16, 1921, p. 911; "Report of the Board of Officers, Springfield Armory," Jan. 12, 1922, National Archives, Record Group 177, Records of the chief of arms, Infantry Board Reports, Box 36, File 570; "Details of the Larsen All-Metal Attack Plane," *Army and Navy Journal*, Nov. 5, 1921, pp. 218, 221, 225; Helmer, pp. 70–77; Sharpe, p. 1109; "To Stop Automobile Bandits," *Literary Digest,* July 15, 1922, p. 24; "New York Letter," *Philadelphia Inquirer*, May 11, 1922; "New Goods and Improvements," *Hardware Dealers' Magazine,* April 1, 1921; Hill, p. 100.

Quotes: "nearly mechanical perfection": *Army and Navy Journal,* April 16, 1921, p. 911.

"be handled by officers": Helmer, p. 72.

"was perforated til it looked like": *Literary Digest,* July 15, 1922, p. 24.

"converted a solid-looking": *Philadelphia Inquirer,* May 11, 1922.

"the latest money-making things": *Hardware Dealers' Magazine,* April 1, 1921.

"So it came to pass": Helmer, p. 77.

"On the Side of Law and Order": Hill, p. 100.

Chapter 5: Rebellion

Just weeks after the first guns: Statement of William E. McNarney, June 24, 1921, National Archives, Bureau of Investigation microfilm, BOI files 52-505, M-1085, Reel 910; Roy C. McHenry, "Memorandum for Assistant Attorney General Crim," Oct. 4, 1921, National Archives, U.S. Department of Justice files, RG 60, File 52-205, Box 172; "600 Machine Guns Supposed for Irish Taken on Ship Here," *New York Times,* June 16, 1921; "Seized Irish Guns Provide Mysteries Within a Mystery," *New York Times,* June 17, 1921.

For centuries, Ireland: "Wars & Conflict: 1916 Easter Rising," www.BBC.co.uk; Patrick J. Jung, "British Diplomats and Irish Gun Runners in the United States During the Anglo-Irish War 1920–21," *Bulletin of the Military Historical Society,* Feb. 1997, p. 132; Charles Dalton, Bureau of Military History Statement by Witness, Document No. 454, www.bureauofmilitaryhistory.ie; "Volleys and Bombs: Three Soldiers Wounded," *Irish Independent,* June 17, 1921; J. Bowyer Bell, "The Thompson Submachine Gun in Ireland, 1921," *Irish Sword,* Winter 1967, pp. 106–107.

How did a brand-new automatic weapon: Patrick J. Jung, "The Thompson Submachine Gun During the Anglo-Irish War: The New Evidence," *Irish Sword,* Winter 1998, unpaged; Bell, pp. 99–103; McHenry memo, pp. 1–4; Helmer, pp. 55–63; Vincent Byrne, Bureau of Military History Statement by Witness, Document No. 423; Tom Barry, *Guerilla Days in Ireland,* pp. 257–258; "Seized Irish Guns Provide

Mysteries Within a Mystery," *New York Times,* June 17, 1921; "Claimant of Guns Bound for Ireland Under Espionage," *New York World,* June 17, 1921; "U.S. Gun Seizure Foils Sinn Fein Campaign Plans," *Atlanta Constitution,* June 18, 1921.

Quotes: "see what the Irish crowd": McHenry memo, p. 3.

"I would miss": Barry, p. 257.

"a day replete with," "pronounced Irish accent," and "Surely you mean": *New York Times,* June 17, 1921.

"For the present": *Atlanta Constitution,* June 18, 1921.

Marcellus Thompson crafted: McHenry memo, pp. 1–11; Auto-Ordnance weekly sales records, U.S. Department of Justice files, RG 60, File 52-205, Box 172; Barry Denenberg, *The True Story of J. Edgar Hoover and the FBI,* pp. 26–28; Memos to and from Hoover, National Archives, Bureau of Investigation microfilm, BOI files 52-505, M-1085, Reel 910.

Quotes: "To begin with": McHenry memo, pp. 9–11.

"Speed": Denenberg, p. 26.

Meanwhile, in the United States: Patrick McCrea, Col. Padraig O. Conchubhair, and George Nolan, Bureau of Military History Statement by Witnesses, Documents No. 413, 813, and 596; "Train Bombed," *Irish Times,* July 9, 1921; "Train Attacked Near Clondalkin," *Irish Times,* July 12, 1921; "Harvey's Son-In-Law Held in Arms Plot," *New York Times,* June 20, 1922; "Eight Indicted as Gun Runners to Irish Rebels," *New York World,* June 20, 1922; Letter to William J. Helmer from J. Walter Yeagley, assistant attorney general, and memos from Jan. 16, 1923, and Nov. 1925, National Archives, DOJ files, RG 60, File 52-205, Box 172; Helmer, pp. 64–66, 157–158; McHenry memo, p. 3; Jung, "The Thompson submachine gun," (unpaged), Tom Mahon, "Up Kerry! Up the IRA," *History Ireland,* Sept./Oct. 2010, pp. 38–39; Eickhoff, p. 15; Hill, pp. 19, 139; Brian Albrecht, "Famed Tommy Gun of Roaring '20s and World War II Was Designed in Cleveland," Cleveland.com, Aug. 1, 2011.

Quotes: "Of course, we would not": *New York Times,* June 20, 1922.

"The future": Eickhoff, p. 15.

Chapter 6: The Chicago Piano

In the early fall of 1924: "Arms Bought in Denver for Chicago War," *Rocky Mountain News*, Nov. 12, 1924; John Kobler, *Capone,* pp. 128–129, 134–138; Maureen M'Kernan, "In $10,000 Casket Dean Lies in State," *Chicago Daily Tribune,* Nov. 13, 1924; Jonathan Eig, *Get Capone,* pp. 33–35, 38–40; "Vote Against More Police and Pay Raise," *Chicago Daily Tribune*, Jan. 13, 1925; Robert J. Schoenberg, *Mr. Capone,* pp. 140–141, 145, 150–152; Helmer, pp. 82–84; "Rapid-Firing Gun Spits in Gang Strife," *Los Angeles Times,* Oct. 6, 1925; "Hunt McErlane and Soltis in Saloon Shooting," *Chicago Daily Tribune,* Feb. 11, 1926; "Gangsters Turn Machine Gun on William McSwiggin," *Chicago Daily Tribune,* April 28, 1926; Illinois Association for Criminal Justice, "Illinois Crime Survey, 1929," pp. 828, 831, 834, 1091; Fred D. Pasley, *Al Capone,* p. 131; "Murder and Graft in Chicago Attributed to Beer Wars," *New York Herald Tribune*, May 2, 1926; "Kill Policeman Hunting Slayer of McSwiggin," *New York Herald Tribune*, April 30, 1926; "Special Jurors to Begin Inquiry in Gang Murder," *Times-Picayune* (New Orleans, LA), May 3, 1926.

Quotes: "Got those in" and "The struggle for power": *Rocky Mountain News*, Nov. 12, 1924.

"The bullets were": Helmer, p. 83.

"the hanging prosecutor": *Chicago Daily Tribune,* April 28, 1926.

"car speeding away": Illinois Association for Criminal Justice, "Illinois Crime Survey, 1929," p. 831.

"were of the copper": *Chicago Daily Tribune,* April 28, 1926.

At the Auto-Ordnance office: Helmer, pp. 85–87; "Terrible Power of Gang's Gun Told by Maker," *Chicago Daily Tribune*, April 29, 1926; William G. Shepherd, "Machine Gun Madness," *Collier's*, Dec. 11, 1926; "Man Who Sold Gangster Guns Fears Vengeance If He Tells," *Atlanta Constitution*, May 1, 1926; "Trace Machine Gun in Killng," *Los Angeles Times,* May 3, 1926; "Crime Jury Gets M'Swiggin Facts; Ends Work Today," *Chicago Daily Tribune*, June 4, 1926; Eig, pp. 40–44; Schoenberg, pp. 152–156.

Quotes: "We designed": "Terrible Power of Gang's Gun Told by Maker," *Chicago Daily Tribune*, April 29, 1926.

"If I tell you": "Man Who Sold Gangster Guns Fears Vengeance If He Tells," *Atlanta Constitution*, May 1, 1926.

A half-dozen shootings: "Chicago Police Mystified in Machine Gun Murders," *Los Angeles Times*, April 29, 1926; Pasley, pp. 117–119; Schoenberg, pp. 159–163; Eig, pp. 50–53, 73, 76–79; "2 Slain, 3 Wounded with Machine Gun in Chicago Street," *Washington Post*, Oct. 12, 1926; "46 Slain This Year in Gang Booze War," *Chicago Daily Tribune*, Oct. 12, 1926; Kobler, p. 96; "Prohibition in Chicago," *Chicago Daily Tribune,* Oct. 13, 1926; Patricia Dougherty, "Booze: A Woman Reporter's Inside Story of the Most Extraordinary Situation in the United States," *Cosmopolitan*, April 1927, p. 34.

Quotes: "than a man could": *Los Angeles Times*, April 29, 1926.

"It's a wonder": Eig, p. 52.

"to the streets": *Chicago Daily Tribune,* Oct. 13, 1926.

"killing was unnecessary": *Cosmopolitan*, April 1927, p. 34.

"I don't want": Eig, p. 77.

"Gangland killings": Eig, p. 79.

Chapter 7: Wild Tigers

For all the killings: "Marines Will Be Called to Guard Mail Trucks," *Trenton Evening Times*, Oct. 16, 1926; "1,200 Guards Leave Quantico," *New York Times*, Oct. 22, 1926; "Machine Guns for Mails," *New York Times,* Oct. 27, 1926; Helmer, pp. 96–97 (the guns given to the Marines to guard the mails would later be used by them in conflicts in China and Nicaragua); "Farmers Join Cops in Hunt for Outlaws," *Newark Star-Eagle*, Oct. 15, 1926, p. 1; "Killer Cunniffe Slayer Is Identified by Police as New York Burglar," *Trenton Evening Times*, Nov. 1, 1926; " 'Killer' Cunniffe Is Slain in Detroit; Three Others Dead," *New York Times*, Nov. 1, 1926; "Killer-Bandit Dies in Fight Over Loot That Ends 4 Lives," *Washington Post*, Nov. 1, 1926; "Crowley Identified as Mail Slayer," *New York Times*, Nov. 3, 1926.

Quote: "to shoot to kill": *New York Times*, Oct. 22, 1926.

The horror and outrage: "How Do Killers Get Their Machine Guns? Is Question," *Newark Star-Eagle*, Oct. 15, 1926, p. 8; Kennett and Anderson, pp. 174–75, 181–82, 194, 199–201; Peter Duffy, "100 Years Ago, the Shot That Spurred New York's Gun-Control Law," *New York Times*, Jan. 23, 2011; "Bar Hidden Weapons on Sullivan's Plea," *New York Times*, May 11, 1911; "New Law to Curb Sale of Machine Guns Is Drafted," *Chicago Daily Tribune*, May 9, 1928; Owen P. White, "Machine Guns for Sale," *Collier's*, Dec. 4, 1926; William G. Shepherd, "Machine Gun Madness," *Collier's*, Dec. 11, 1926.

Quotes: "a diabolical engine of death" to "That makes three": *Collier's*, Dec. 11, 1926.

By 1925, Auto-Ordnance had sold: Helmer, pp. 68, 74, 88–89; "Suspect in Rum War Arrested," *Los Angeles Times,* Aug. 5, 1925; "Rum Crew Is Blamed for Death," *Trenton Sunday Times-Advertiser,* April 5, 1925; "One Killed, 2 Hurt in Gangster Attack With Machine Gun," *Seattle Daily Times,* Feb. 25, 1927; "Reveals Gun Sales to 'Bootlegger King,'" *New York Times,* Sept. 7, 1928; "Two Detroit Men Slain by Machine Guns," *Belvidere Daily Republican,* March 28, 1927; William J. Helmer and Rick Mattix, *The Complete Public Enemy Almanac,* pp. 174–175; Shepherd, *Collier's;* White, *Collier's*; Hill, p. 225.

Quotes: "you're a" and "There wasn't anything": Shepherd, *Collier's*.

"We can't turn": White, *Collier's*.

"As you have asserted": Hill, p. 225.

Chapter 8: Valentines and Violins

The Tommy guns in Chicago: "Find Massacre Gang's Target Range on Island," *Chicago Daily Tribune,* May 1, 1929; "Buyer of Six Machines Guns Traced in Quiz," *Chicago Daily Tribune,* April 20, 1929; "Two Seized as Purchasers of Machine Guns," *Chicago Daily Tribune,* May 3, 1929, p. 4; Hill, p. 223; Karen Blumenthal, *Bootleg,* pp. 1–3, 103–105; Schoenberg, pp. 207–213; Eig, pp. 187–190; Some accounts say five men entered and exited the warehouse; Helmer, pp. 92, 121; "Chicago Gangs

Own 500 Machines Guns, Stege Says," *Chicago Daily Tribune*, May 13, 1929; Schoenberg, p. 226.

Quotes: "there was no law": *Chicago Daily Tribune*, May 13, 1929.

"No": Schoenberg, p. 226.

To help crack the massacre case: C. W. Muehlberger, "Col. Calvin Hooker Goddard, 1891–1955," *Journal of Criminal Law and Criminology,* Vol. 46, issue 1, pp. 103–104; "Chicago Gangs Own 500 Machines Guns, Stege Says," *Chicago Daily Tribune,* May 13, 1929; "New Law to Curb the Sale of Machine Guns Is Drafted," *Chicago Daily Tribune,* May 9, 1928; Parke Brown, "Governor Kills Bill to Outlaw Machine Guns," *Chicago Daily Tribune,* June 27, 1929; Schoenberg, pp. 226–228; Eig, pp. 248–250, 365–367.

Quotes: "I told him": *Chicago Daily Tribune*, May 13, 1929;

"may be sold": *Chicago Daily Tribune,* May 9, 1928.

The year 1929: Helmer, pp. 135–145; Hill, pp. 212, 219–220; "Munitions: Chopper," *Time,* June 26, 1939; *The National Cyclopaedia of American Biography*, pp. 298–299.

In the early 1930s: "The American Experience: The Era of Gangster Films, 1930–1935," www.pbs.org; Gregory D. Black, "Hollywood Censored: The Production Code Administration and the Hollywood Film Industry, 1930–1940," *Film History,* Vol. 3, No. 3, p. 170; Alan L. Gansberg, *Little Caesar,* pp. 46, 48; "Robbers Fire, Panic in Café," *Chicago Daily Tribune,* Nov. 22, 1916; Herman D. Hancock, "Ex Policeman Admits Donaldson Murder," *Atlanta Constitution,* March 7, 1927; "Machine Gunners Hold Up Train in City: Rob Banker," *Chicago Herald Examiner,* March 7, 1929; "Hold Up Coach of Train; Rob Joliet Banker," *Chicago Daily Tribune,* March 7, 1929; "Offer $10,000 for Checks Taken in Holdup on Train," *Chicago Daily Tribune*, April 8, 1929; The Stege photo with the violin case did not show up in a review of the *Chicago Daily News* for 1927 and around the time of the train robbery; it isn't clear that it ever ran in the paper; *The Doorway to Hell*, MGM Warner Archive Collection, 1930; Frank Miller, *Censored Hollywood,* p. 56.

Quotes: "the public preoccupation": Gansberg, p. 48.

"I'm going out": *The Doorway to Hell*, MGM Warner Archive Collection, 1930.

Chapter 9: Attack and Intimidation

While Chicago officials seemed to look: "Child Slain, 4 Shot as Gangsters Fire on Beer War Rival," *New York Times,* July 29, 1931; "5 Children Shot in Street as Beer Guerillas in Car Turn Machine Gun on Foe," *New York Herald Tribune*, July 29, 1931; "Gang Murder of Boy Stirs Public Anger," *New York Times,* July 30, 1931; "Aroused City Spurs Hunt in Child Murder," *New York Herald Tribune,* July 30, 1931 (in some accounts, the child in the carriage was reported as four years old and "Vengalli" was spelled "Vengali"); "Machine Gun Ban Aim of Albany Bill," *New York Times,* "Crime Curb Bills Urged at Albany," *New York Times,"* Sept. 17, 1931; "Roosevelt Cites Own Case to Show Gun-Permit Dangers," *New York Times,* Sept. 3, 1931; "Roosevelt Delayed on Relief Program," *New York Times,* Sept. 23, 1931; "Coll Is Acquitted; Case to Seabury," *New York Times,* Dec. 29, 1931; "Coll Is Shot Dead in a Phone Booth by Rival Gunmen," *New York Times,* Feb. 8, 1932; "Coll Betrayed to His Slayer by Bodyguard," *Trenton Evening Times*, Feb. 8, 1932.

Quotes: "sharp crackling" and "their terrorism": "Child Slain, 4 Shot as Gangsters Fire on Beer War Rival," *New York Times,* July 29, 1931.

"damnable": "Gang Murder of Boy Stirs Public Anger," *New York Times,* July 30, 1931.

"There is no good reason": "Crime Curb Bills Urged at Albany," *New York Times,"* Sept. 17, 1931.

"Turn around, Vincent": "Coll Betrayed to His Slayer by Bodyguard," *Trenton Evening Times*, Feb. 8, 1932.

In 1933, as the Great Depression: Orville Dwyer, "Strike Grows; 3,500 Miners Out in State," *Chicago Daily Tribune*, Dec. 11, 1929; Helmer, pp. 144–149; "Violations of Free Speech and Rights of Labor," Report of the Committee on Education and Labor, pursuant to S. Res. 266, 76th Congress, First Session, 1939, Report No. 6, Part 3, pp. 8–12, 42–46, 68–72, 101–102, 138–139, 182–190; "Violations of Free Speech and Rights of Labor," Hearings before a Subcommittee of the Committee on Education and Labor, United States Senate, 75th Congress, First Session, S. Res. 266, Part 7, pp. 2433–2436, 2466–2467, 2609; Tonya Bolden, *FDR's Alphabet Soup,* pp. 27, 42–46; "Violations of Free Speech and Rights of Labor," Hearings before a Subcommittee of the Committee on Education and Labor, United States Senate, 75th Congress, Second Session, S. Res. 266, Part 15-D, pp. 7005–7007; "Heavily Armed Citizens Guard Ambridge," *Morning Herald* (Uniontown, PA), Oct. 6, 1933, p. 1.

Quotes: "The same as police": Report of the Committee on Education and Labor, p. 11.

"is the gangster's weapon": Report of the Committee on Education and Labor, p. 72.

"That is a part of": Hearings before a Subcommittee, 75th Congress, p. 2433.

"There is only one 'out' ": Report of the Committee on Education and Labor, p. 102.

"wanted 200 shotguns": Report of the Committee on Education and Labor, p. 138.

"we do not": Report of the Committee on Education and Labor, p. 46.

Chapter 10: The War on Crime

Prohibition had spawned a generation: Bryan Burrough, *Public Enemies*, pp. 19–21, 40–55, 447; Helmer and Mattix, pp. 52–53; Michael Wallis, *Pretty Boy,* pp. 68–69, 144, 187, 292, 316–317; Wallis says Floyd's friends from home also called him Choc, reflecting his youthful fondness for a local home brew known as Choctaw beer; "Oklahoma's 'Bandit King,' " *Literary Digest*, Dec. 10, 1932, pp. 26–27. Curt Gentry, *J. Edgar Hoover*, p. 167–168; "Kansas City Massacre—Charles Arthur 'Pretty Boy' Floyd" www.fbi.gov/about-us/history/famous-cases/kansas-city-massacre-pretty-boy-floyd; "Massacre in Kansas City," *New York Times*, June 18, 1933; Helmer, pp. 106–108; John Toland, *The Dillinger Days,* pp. 52–59; Robert Unger, *The Union Station Massacre,* pp. 224–229; "The Machine-Gun Challenge to the Nation," *Literary Digest,* July 1, 1933, p. 34.

Quotes: "Oklahoma bad men": Burrough, p. 20.

"I have robbed": Burrough, p. 21.

"Up! Up!" Burrough, p. 49. Also, www.fbi.gov/about-us/history/famous-cases /kansas-city-massacre-pretty-boy-floyd.

"The Machine-Gun Challenge": *Literary Digest,* July 1, 1933, p. 34.

The election of Franklin Delano Roosevelt: Bolden, pp. 26–27; "Cummings Asks Law to Aid Fight on Gangs," *New York Times,* July 2, 1933; "Will Aid Cummings in War on Gangs," *New York Times,* July 4, 1933; "Roosevelt Will Back War on Kidnappers With Larger Fund and Many More Agents," *New York Times,* July 26, 1933; Burrough, pp. 9–15, 58–59; Denenberg, pp. 30–38; "Welcome to the World of Fingerprints," and "The Birth of the FBI Lab" from "The FBI and the American Gangster, 1924–1938," www.fbi.gov; J. Edgar Hoover, "Crime Trap," *American Magazine,* Nov. 1933, p. 66, from National Archives at College Park, MD, Records of the Federal Bureau of Investigation, Record Group 65, Hoover Scrapbooks, Box 3; John F. Fox, "The Birth of the FBI's Technical Laboratory—1924–1935," www.fbi.gov; Ray Tucker, "Hist! Who's That?" *Collier's,* Aug. 19, 1933, pp. 14–15, 49, National Archives, Hoover Scrapbooks, Box 3.

Quotes: "some method of": *New York Times,* July 2, 1933.

"a declaration of war": *New York Times,* July 4, 1933.

"secret federal police" and "appetite for publicity": *Collier's,* Aug. 19, 1933, pp. 15, 49.

Late on the night of July 22: Burrough, pp. 68–75, 79–84, 87–94, 116–119, 120–125, 129–134; Stanley Hamilton, *Machine Gun Kelly's Last Stand,* pp. 67–75; Helmer, pp. 108–110; "The Urschel Kidnapping" video on Richard Green, "Gangsters, G-Men, and Archivists," The Unwritten Record blog, blogs.archives.gov; Hoover, *Persons in Hiding,* pp. 145–166; "George 'Machine Gun' Kelly," www.fbi.gov; Frank C. Waldrop, "The Urschel Kidnapers' Mistake," *Washington-Herald,* Feb. 8, 1934,

National Archives, Hoover Scrapbooks, Box 4; "Kidnapper Kelly Dies in U.S. Prison," *New York Times,* July 18, 1954.

Quotes: "probably the most inept": Burrough, p. 72.

"banking business": Hamilton, p. 71.

"[S]he rode": Hoover, p. 150.

"Kelly is most proficient": Burrough, p. 74.

"I been waiting": Burrough, p. 132.

"Don't shoot, G-men!": Burrough, p. 133, also "George 'Machine Gun' Kelly," www.fbi.gov.

"Honey, I guess": Burrough, p. 134.

Chapter 11: Cops and Robbers

When Al Capone wanted powerful guns: Burrough, pp. 94–97, 125, 135–142; Toland, pp. 5–14, 71–74, 105–132.

Quote: "We're Michigan officers": "Kill Ohio Sheriff, Free His Prisoner," *New York Times*, Oct. 13, 1933.

In the week after: Burrough, pp. 142–44, 153–167, 178; Toland, pp. 132–134, 142–159; In March 2014, the Tommy gun stolen in Auburn, Indiana, was returned to the town, after spending more than thirty years in Tucson, Arizona, and an additional forty-eight years at FBI headquarters ("Tommy Gun Stolen by Dillinger Gang Returned to Indiana Town," *Chicago Tribune,* March 7, 2014); "Indiana Mobilizes 2,000 in Crime War," *New York Times,* Oct. 29, 1933; "50 Police Led by Stege Hunt Convict Gang," *Chicago Daily Tribune,* Dec. 19, 1933.

Quote: "the desperados who": *New York Times,* Oct. 29, 1933.

As the new year began: Blumenthal, *Six Days in October,* pp. 138–142; Elliott Thurston, "Perpetuation of NRA Urged, But Address Lacks Details," *Washington Post,* Jan. 4, 1934; " 'New Deal' Is Here to Stay, President Tells Congress," *New York Times*, Jan. 4, 1934; "Text of Roosevelt's Message Read to Congress," *New York Times,* Jan. 4, 1934; R. S. Thornburgh, "The War on Crime," *New York Times,* March 4, 1934; "Rigid Control of Guns Urged to Balk Gangs," *Washington Post,* March 21, 1934;

"Would Register All Machine Guns," *Sun* (Baltimore), March 21, 1934; Burrough, pp. 186–189, 199–205; Toland, pp. 173–192; "Dillinger Caught on Fireman's Tip," *New York Times,* Jan. 26, 1934.

Quote: "unethical" and "criminal": *New York Times,* Jan. 4, 1934.

A few days later: "Dillinger Is Back in Indiana Jail," *New York Times,* Jan. 31, 1934; Burrough, pp. 206–212, 234–240, 247–249, footnote on pp. 242–243; Toland, pp. 193–197, 205–216, 245; " 'Only Have One Bad Habit—Robbing Banks,' Dillinger Says," *Washington Post,* Feb. 1, 1934; "Holdup Victims Name Dillinger as Police Killer," *Chicago Daily Tribune,* Feb. 1, 1934; "Topics of the Times," *New York Times,* Feb. 2, 1934; "Dillinger Escapes Jail; Using a Wooden Pistol He Locks Guards in Cell," *New York Times,* March 4, 1934.

Quotes: "My only bad habit": *Washington Post,* Feb. 1, 1934.

"Are you glad" through "I stick to": Burrough, p. 207.

"I locked eight deputys": Toland, p. 245.

"a daring escape": *New York Times,* March 4, 1934.

Chapter 12: Public Enemies

Many, many miles away from John Dillinger: "Federal 'Teeth' Asked in Gang War," *New York Times,* March 20, 1934; "Roosevelt Will Direct Drive to Rid Nation of Criminals," *Washington Post,* March 31, 1934; "Homer Cummings Diaries," March 23, 1924, Library of Congress, 17.477, microfilm roll 1: 1919–1936; Raymond Moley and Celeste Jedel, "The Gentleman Who Does Not Yield Hatton Sumners, Dallas Diogenes," *Saturday Evening Post,* May 10, 1941, p. 102; Elmore Whitehurst, "Hatton Sumners: His Life and Public Service, an Extended Biographical Sketch," from www.hattonsumners.org; Raymond Moley, *27 Masters of Politics,"* (New York: Funk & Wagnalls Company, 1949), pp. 266–267.

Quotes: "that has more people": *New York Times,* March 20, 1934.

"on a minute's": *Washington Post,* March 31, 1934.

"and try to get him": "Homer Cummings Diaries," March 23, 1924, Library of Congress, 17.477, microfilm roll 1: 1919–1936.

"that he did not think": Elmore Whitehurst, "Hatton Sumners," from www
.hattonsumners.org.

"I'd just like to see": *Saturday Evening Post,* May 10, 1941, p. 102 (The account here reflects parts of two versions of this story, one of which includes a profanity).

Never one to dawdle: Burrough, pp. 99–103, 243–261, 267–274, 281–322; Toland, pp. 217–239, 245–249, 251–255, 261–284; Gentry, p. 171; "Dillinger Escapes Posses After Two Running Fights," *New York Times,* April 24, 1934; "Gibe at Raid on Dillinger," *New York Times,* April 25, 1934; "National Affairs: Bad Man at Large," *Time,* May 7, 1934.

Quotes: "had a baby face": Burrough, p. 103.

"atrocious bungling": Burrough, p. 272.

"All we want": Burrough, p. 303.

"bungle of the revenooers": *New York Times,* April 25, 1934.

Chapter 13: Recoil

Somehow, some way, the Roosevelt administration: "New Dillinger Killings Stir the President and He Asks Quick Action on Crime Bills," *New York Times,* April 24, 1934; "Crime Bills Sped by Dillinger Hunt," *New York Times,* April 25, 1934; "Cummings Asks Airplanes," *New York Times,* April 25, 1934; "7 Anticrime Bills Receive House Backing," *Washington Post,* May 15, 1934; "Boy Is 'Governor' for an Hour," *New York Times,* April 5, 1934; Burrough, p. 345; "Roosevelt Opens Attack on Crime, Signing Six Bills as 'Challenge,'" *New York Times,* May 19, 1934.

Quotes: "Public opinion demands": *New York Times,* April 25, 1934.

"governor for an hour": *New York Times,* April 5, 1934.

"Law enforcement and": *New York Times,* May 19, 1934.

"looking to the safeguarding": *New York Times,* April 25, 1934.

From the very start: In 1919, the federal government assessed an excise tax on firearms and ammunition, among other goods, to raise revenue after World War I, not to reduce gun sales. That revenue now goes to wildlife restoration programs;

"Criminals Buy Weapons Easily, Evidence Shows," *Christian Science Monitor*, May 8, 1934; Carol Skalnik Leff and Mark H. Leff, "The Politics of Ineffectiveness," pp. 52–55; Robert J. Spitzer, *The Politics of Gun Control*, pp. 34–36; Stephen P. Halbrook, *That Every Man Be Armed*, pp. 76–81; "A More Perfect Union: The Creation of the U.S. Constitution," www.archives.gov; Saul Cornell, *A Well Regulated Militia*, pp. 5, 58–70, 175–197; Kennett and Anderson, pp. 51–54, 75, 81, 203–212; Donald Curtis Brown, *The Great Gun-Toting Controversy, 1865–1910*, pp. 11, 14, 21–24, 113–114, 437–438; Chris Kyle, with William Doyle, *American Gun,* pp. 77–83; Adam Winkler, *Gun Fight,* pp. 134–145, 196–217; Susan Campbell Bartoletti, *They Called Themselves the K.K.K.,* pp. 121–130.

Quotes: "The right of the people," "A well regulated militia," and "A well regulated Militia": Spitzer, pp. 34–36, and Halbrook, pp. 76, 81.

"every free, able-bodied": Kennett and Anderson, p. 81.

Since the mid-1920s: Trefethen and Serven, pp. 215–233; Jeffrey L. Rodengen, *NRA*, pp. 83–98; Hearings before a Subcommittee of the Committee on Commerce, United States Senate, 73rd Congress, Second Session, on S. 885, S. 2258, and S. 3680, May 28 and 29, 1934, pp. 8–11, 16–17, 31, 45, 72–74; Hearings before the Committee on Ways and Means, House of Representatives, 73rd Congress, Second Session, on H.R. 9066, April 15, 16 and May 14, 15, and 16, 1934, pp. 40–41, 53–57, 63; Helmer, pp. 120–121, 124–126; "Anti-Arms Group Wins Its Battle on Machine Guns," *Christian Science Monitor,* May 10, 1934; "Law to Disarm Gangsters Opposed by Men Who Want Free Right to Buy Pistols," *Christian Science Monitor,* May 16, 1934; "Club Women Join Battle to Block Firearms Sales," *Christian Science Monitor,* May 25, 1934; "Club-Women Mapping War on Gangsters," *Literary Digest,* June 16, 1934, p. 19; "National Firearms Act," 48 Stat. 1236, 73rd Congress, Sess. 2, Chap. 757, June 26, 1934.

Quotes: "Once on the books": Hearings before a Subcommittee of the Committee on Commerce, p. 73.

"You can be just as severe": Hearings before a Subcommittee of the Committee on Commerce, p. 31.

"Automobiles are a much more": Hearings before the Committee on Ways and Means, p. 54.

"Is it too much": "Law to Disarm Gangsters Opposed by Men Who Want Free Right to Buy Pistols," *Christian Science Monitor,* May 16, 1934.

"two million American club-women": "Club-Women Mapping War on Gangsters," *Literary Digest,* June 16, 1934, p. 19.

Chapter 14: Reload

Ultimately, John Dillinger's appetite for women: Toland, pp. 301–331; 340–341; Burrough, pp. 170–171, 260, 342–343, 362–416, 452, 446–447, 457–468, 473–483, 521, 548; News accounts from the time list Dillinger as thirty-two years old, though he was born in 1903, Anna Sage's name was sometimes spelled "Ana"; "Kill Dillinger Here," *Chicago Daily Tribune,* July 23, 1934; Wallis, pp. 288–289, 318–339; "Slain Agents Fired 60 Shots at Nelson," *New York Times,* Nov. 29, 1934.

Quote: "grieved beyond words": *New York Times,* Nov. 29, 1934.

Al Capone, the most violent: "Cummings Says Slaying of Dillinger Is 'Gratifying as Well as Reassuring,'" *New York Times,* July 23, 1934; Russell Owen, "Men Who Track Down the Public Enemy," *New York Times,* Oct. 28, 1934; Jack Alexander, "Profiles: The Director—I" *New Yorker,* Sept. 25, 1937, p. 21; Basil Gallagher, "Government Spent Half Million to Hunt Down Criminal Who Did Not Like to Hide," *Press-Scimitar* (Memphis, TN), July 1934, from National Archives at College Park, FBI files, Record Group 65, Hoover Scrapbooks, Box 4; Milton S. Mayer, "Myth of the G-Men," *Forum,* Sept. 1935, pp. 144–148.

Quotes: "exceedingly gratifying": *New York Times,* July 23, 1934.

"The only thing": *New York Times,* Oct. 28, 1934.

"shoot to kill": *Forum,* Sept. 1935, p. 145.

Still, as the bureau: Stephen Vaughn, "The Devil's Advocate: Will H. Hays and the Campaign to Make Movies Respectable," *Indiana Magazine of History,* Vol. 101, No. 2 (June 2005), p. 126; Gregory D. Black, "Hollywood Censored: The Production

Code Administration and the Hollywood Film Industry," *Film History*, Vol. 3, No. 3 (1989), pp. 167–189; Geoffrey Shurlock, "The Motion Picture Production Code," *Annals of the American Academy of Political and Social Science*, Nov. 1947, pp. 141–142; Miller, pp. 56, 84–93; "Hays Office Forbids All Film Productions Dealing with Exploits of John Dillinger," *Los Angeles Times*, March 21, 1934; Powers, *Secrecy and Power*, pp. 200–201; Burrough, pp. 517–518; Denenberg, p. 70.

Chapter 15: The End of an Era

Something else unexpected happened: "Violations of Free Speech and Rights of Labor," Hearings before a Subcommittee of the Committee on Education and Labor, 75th Congress, First Sess., part 7, p. 2432; "Machine Gun Sales Curbed By New Law," *New York Times,* Dec. 25, 1934; "Registry of One Weapon Purchase in Year Shows Gangsters Flouting Firearms Act," *New York Times,* Nov. 6, 1936; "Urges Firearms Act to Include All Kinds," *New York Times,* May 5, 1937; Carl Brent Swisher, editor, *Selected Papers of Homer Cummings,* pp. 88–89; Leff and Leff, p. 52; Katherine Kaufer Christoffel, "Firearm Injuries: Epidemic Then, Endemic Now," *American Journal of Public Health*, April 2007, accessed online; "Powder Smoke: Random Shots," *American Rifleman,* Aug. 1934, p. 4; "Federal Agent Is Ordered Held for Grand Jury for Murder of Woman in Raid," *Joplin News Herald,* July 16, 1934; Alexander DeConde, *Gun Violence in America,* pp. 146–149; Kennett and Anderson, pp. 79, 211–112.

Quotes: "relatively few innocent": *American Rifleman,* Aug. 1934, p. 4.

"No honest man": Swisher, p. 89.

In the 1930s: "History of Submachine Guns, 1921–1945," Small Arms Division, Industrial Service Ordnance Department, Compiled by Mr. W. H. Davis, Capt. Andrew J. Gleason, pp. 3–5, National Archives at College Park, MD, Records of the Office of the Chief of Ordnance, RG 156; "Report of Test by the Department of Experiment, The Infantry School, Fort Benning, Ga.," Dec. 14, 1931, National Archives at College Park, MD, Records of the Chiefs of Arms, RG 177; Helmer, pp. 161–181; Hill, pp. 273–279; "Munitions: Chopper," *Time,* June 26, 1939.

Quotes: "had become very fond": "Report of Test by the Department of Experiment, The Infantry School, Fort Benning, Ga.," National Archives, p. 12.

"the deadliest weapon": *Time,* June 26, 1939.

"the T.S.M.G. has": Helmer, p. 178.

"I often think of you": Helmer, p. 179.

Epilogue: Legacy

The Thompson submachine gun may have seen: Helmer, pp. 182–186, 192, 212; Davis and Gleason, "History of Submachine Guns: 1921–1945," pp. 3, 10–11, 28, 51, 56; Auto-Ordnance, www.auto-ordnance.com; "John Edgar Hoover" and "New FBI Director," www.fbi.gov; Denenberg, pp. 73–76; Mark Mazzetti, "Burglars Who Took on F.B.I. Abandon Shadows," *New York Times,* Jan. 7, 2014; "The Truth About J. Edgar Hoover," *Time*, Dec. 22, 1975; Congress can extend an FBI director's term— Robert S. Mueller III served twelve years.

Quotes: "gained considerable popularity": Davis and Gleason, p. 56.

"grease gun": Helmer, p. 186.

Though long gone: Philip J. Cook, draft of "The Great American Gun War: Notes from Four Decades in the Trenches," provided by the author; "History of Gun-Control Legislation," *Washington Post,* Dec. 22, 2012; DeConde, pp. 185–187, 229–230; Winkler, pp. 65–68, 256–258; Joel Achenbach, Scott Higham, and Sari Horwitz, "How NRA's True Believers Converted a Marksmanship Group into a Mighty Gun Lobby," *Washington Post,* Jan. 12, 2013; Gun laws and other details accessed at www.gunpolicy. org/firearms/regionunited-states; "ATF National Firearms Act Handbook," Bureau of Alcohol, Tobacco, Firearms and Explosives, U.S. Department of Justice, 2009, www.atf.gov, Chap. 1; Brad Plummer, "Everything You Need to Know About the Assault Weapons Ban, in One Post," www.washingtonpost.com, Dec. 12, 2012; Philip J. Cook and Kristin A. Goss, *The Gun Debate*, p. 80; "The Writers Guide to Firearms and Ammunition" and "Background Information on So-Called 'Assault Weapons,'" National Shooting Sports Foundation, www.nssf.org.

Quotes: "We must declare": *Washington Post,* Jan. 12, 2013.

"functionally no different": "Background Information on So-Called 'Assault Weapons,'" National Shooting Sports Foundation, www.nssf.org.

In June 2008: U.S. Supreme Court, *District of Columbia v. Heller,* 554 U.S. 570 (2008); Linda Greenhouse, "Justices, Ruling 5-4, Endorse Personal Right to Own Gun," *New York Times,* June 27, 2008; Robert Barnes, "Justices Reject D.C. Ban on Handgun Ownership," *Washington Post,* June 27, 2008; Matt Pearce, "James Holmes Gets a Trial Date in Aurora, Colo., Massacre," *Los Angeles Times,* Feb. 27, 2014; James Barron, "Children Were All Shot Multiple Times with a Semiautomatic, Officials Say," *New York Times,* Dec. 15, 2012; Gun statistics at www.gunpolicy.org/firearms/region/united-states; Jonathan Stray, "Gun Violence in America: The 13 Key Questions," *The Atlantic,* March 2, 2013; "General Statistics," Insurance Institute for Highway Safety," www.iihs.org; "Protect Children, Not Guns 2013," Children's Defense Fund, accessed online; "Special Report: Firearm Violence, 1993–2011," U.S. Department of Justice, Office of Justice Programs, 2013; Jackie Calmes, "In His Hometown of Chicago, a Policy Speech by Obama Turns Personal," *New York Times,* Feb. 15, 2013; Nikara Johns, "Breaking Cycle of Youth Violence a Challenge," The Red Line Project, www.redlineproject.org; "Dramatic Results of UCAN2012 National Teen Gun Survey Released," UCAN National Teen Gun Survey, April 18, 2012; Cornell, p. 218.

Quotes: "cast doubt": *District of Columbia v. Heller,* 554 U.S. 570 (2008), pp. 54–55.

"The Second Amendment": Cornell, p. 218.

"not unique to": *New York Times,* Feb. 15, 2013.

PICTURE CREDITS

p. vi: *Popular Science*, Oct. 1931; pp. viii, 2, 4: ©Corbis; p. 6: National Park Service, Springfield Armory NHS; p. 8: John Henry Parker, *The Gatlings at Santiago* (Kansas City, Mo.: Hudson-Kimberly Publishing Co., 1898), p. i; p. 10: National Archives (111-SC-90189); p. 11: National Archives (306-ST-505-58-4822); p. 12: Library of Congress; p. 17: Courtesy of the family of Juliet Thompson Debnam (1931–2008), granddaughter of John Thompson; p. 19: Roy Coles Photograph Collection, United States Army Heritage and Education Center, Military History Institute, Carlisle, PA; p. 20: Courtesy U.S. Department of Defense; pp. 22, 25, 26: The American Thompson Reference Collection; p. 27, 28: Library of Congress; pp. 30–31, 33, 36: The American Thompson Reference Collection; p. 38: ©Corbis; pp. 40, 42–43, 46: Bill Helmer Collection; p. 49: Granger, NYC—all rights reserved; p. 51: *Popular Mechanics*, Nov. 1920; p. 53: The American Thompson Reference Collection; p. 56: Courtesy FBI; p. 59: The American Thompson Reference Collection; p. 60: W.D. Hogan, Hogan-Wilson Collection, image courtesy of the National Library of Ireland; p. 63: Chicago History Museum, ICHi-40205; pp. 65, 66, 68: Chicago History Museum, DN-0081396, DN-0080899, DN-0080573, *Chicago Daily News*, photographer; p. 70: ©Hulton-Deutsch Collection/Corbis; p. 72: Chicago History Museum, DN-0082096, *Chicago Daily News*, photographer; p. 73: Chicago History Museum, ICHi-40200; p. 76: ©Corbis; p. 78: By permission of the Estate of Rollin Kirby Post; p. 85: Library of Congress, Prints and Photographs Division, LC-USZ62-123252; p. 87: Chicago History Museum, DN-0090171, *Chicago Daily News*, photographer; p. 89: Library of Congress, Prints & Photographs Division, Clifford Berryman Collection, Oct. 10, 1931; p. 91: ©Warner Brothers; p. 93: Chicago History Museum, DN-0082619; *Chicago Daily News*, photographer; pp. 96, 97: AP Photo; p. 98: *New York Daily News*/Getty Images; p. 101: Harris & Ewing Collection, Library of Congress; p. 103: *Pittsburgh Sun-Telegraph*, Oct. 6, 1933; pp. 108–109: Courtesy FBI; p. 112: Harris & Ewing Collection, Library of Congress; p. 114:

Courtesy FBI; p. 115: Courtesy of *The Oklahoman*; p. 116: AP Photo; p. 120: National Archives (RG 065-HC-10-2); pp. 123, 125: Courtesy FBI; pp. 126–127: ©Hulton-Deutsch Collection/Corbis; p. 128: AP Photo; p. 132: FPG/Getty Images; p. 133: ©Bettmann/Corbis; p. 137: Hatton Sumners Papers, W. R. Poage Legislative Library, Baylor University, Waco, Texas; p. 138: Courtesy FBI; p. 140: ©Bettmann/Corbis; p. 143: AP Photo; pp. 146–147: Bradbury Harrison in *Time* magazine, May 7, 1934; p. 148: National Archives (065-H-206-2); p. 150: Library of Congress; p. 153: Granger, NYC—all rights reserved; p. 155: Milton A. Reckord Papers, Special Collections, University of Maryland Libraries; p. 157: Courtesy General Federation of Women's Clubs; p. 160: Courtesy FBI; pp. 161, 163: AP Photo; p. 164: ©Bettmann/Corbis; p. 166: Courtesy FBI; p. 168: ©Bettmann/Corbis/AP Images; p. 169: National Archives, Clifford Berryman, *The Evening Star* (65 HC-11-32). (Inscription reads: "To J. Edgar Hoover, Who is bent upon taking the joy out of life for gangsters & co. Wish more power to him, C.K. Berryman, *The Evening Star*, 1934); pp. 170–171: Courtesy FBI; pp. 174–175: The American Thompson Reference Collection; p. 179: AP Photo; p. 181: Courtesy of the family of Juliet Thompson Debnam (1931–2008), granddaughter of John Thompson; p. 184: AP Photo/Official British Photo; p. 190: AP Photo/Julio Cortez.

ACKNOWLEDGMENTS

This book began with a note from my editor, Deirdre Langeland, after the tragic shootings in Newtown, Connecticut. There were so many differing views on guns, gun rights, and the Second Amendment, she said. Was there a story there?

I was intrigued, but wasn't quite sure where to begin. I read up on the Second Amendment and the history of guns in the U.S., and after a couple of false starts, I returned to a familiar time period, the 1920s and 1930s. The story of the Thompson submachine gun, the first weapon of war to move to the streets, seemed to parallel many of the issues surrounding guns today.

I am deeply indebted to Deirdre for trusting me to give this a shot, and for her encouragement and always-thoughtful editing. My supportive agent, Susan Cohen, didn't flinch when I proposed a book for young people about guns, and a wonderful team at Roaring Brook, including Simon Boughton, Jill Freshney, Anne Diebel, and Tracy Koontz had my back. I am honored to be a part of this gang.

Many people shared their wisdom and provided assistance, and I owe them all thanks. Philip J. Cook, professor of public policy at Duke University, helped with background information and potential sources. Patrick Jung, a professor at Milwaukee School of Engineering, shared his extensive knowledge of the Irish Tommy gun scandal, as well as documents, photographs, and other resources. Both of them also read a draft.

William F. Atwater, director emeritus of the U.S. Army Ordnance Museum, was incredibly patient in explaining gun mechanics and also provided valuable feedback on the manuscript. Sylvia Schneider helped me get access to the National Firearms Museum Library and Doug Wicklund, senior curator, answered gun-history questions.

My friend Jonathan Eig, author of *Get Capone,* graciously shared a fabulous file of Capone clippings to help me track down early Chicago sightings of the gun. Chicago researcher Christina A. Reynen plowed through months of Chicago newspapers on my behalf, searching for details on Tommy guns and violin cases, and

John Russick, director of curatorial affairs at the Chicago History Museum, answered questions on the subject. Pat Kirby of the Military History Society of Ireland, Tom Ankner of the Newark Public Library, and Noel Kalenian of the Denver Public Library helped find key articles. Abby McCartney also provided crucial research assistance.

Tommy gun experts Bill Helmer and Tracie Hill were incredibly generous in sharing photographs from their extensive collections, and John Fox at the FBI dug up a number of historical images. I am also immensely grateful to Juliet Gross, a granddaughter of Marcellus Thompson, for sharing family photographs.

David Stern and Jenny McCartney took the time to read early drafts and provide crucial feedback, and Patricia Hinton offered a much-needed fresh set of eyes near the end.

Last, I owe enormous thanks to my husband, Scott McCartney; he is the best partner in crime a writer could ever have.

INDEX

Numbers in **bold** indicate pages with illustrations

228